Genealogical Writing in the 21st Century

A Guide to *Register* Style and More

Genealogical Writing in the 21st Century

A Guide to *Register* Style and More

EDITED BY MICHAEL J. LECLERC
AND HENRY B. HOFF

NEW ENGLAND HISTORIC GENEALOGICAL SOCIETY
BOSTON, MASSACHUSETTS

International Standard Book Number: 0-88082-199-X
Library of Congress Control Number: 2006931067

Published by
New England Historic Genealogical Society
101 Newbury Street
Boston, Massachusetts 02116-3007
www.NewEnglandAncestors.org

Printed by Quebecor World, Leominster, Massachusetts.

TABLE OF CONTENTS

PREFACE TO THE SECOND EDITION

Many changes have occurred in the world of genealogical publishing in the four years since the publication of this book's first edition. Some magazines and publishers have closed up shop, but new ones have opened. The Internet has begun to offer more opportunities for publishing genealogical findings, and technology in general has led to changes in best practices.

This second edition of *Genealogical Writing in the 21st Century* has been both revised and expanded. The existing chapters were reviewed and updated to reflect current practices. New chapters illustrate how to "write as you research" and how to use features of the Microsoft® WORD word processing program to help write a compiled genealogy.

Great thanks are due to authors Patricia Law Hatcher, FASG, and Alvy Ray Smith, PhD, for their valuable contributions to the second edition, and to Lynn Betlock; Sharon DeBartolo Carmack, CG; Henry B. Hoff, CG, FASG; Carolyn Sheppard Oakley; and Helen Schatvet Ullmann, CG, FASG, for updating their first-edition chapters. Many thanks also go to Rhonda McClure, Julie Helen Otto, Jean Powers, Scott Steward, and Penny Stratton for their assistance in preparing this book for publication.

A special expression of gratitude goes to Henry Hoff for his contributions to the second edition. His commentary was invaluable, and his support and assistance were crucial to creating this second edition. He is an excellent mentor and role model for all those interested in genealogical publishing.

Michael J. Leclerc
NEHGS Director of Special Projects
July 2006

PREFACE TO THE FIRST EDITION

This guide is the distillation of opinions from many genealogical authors and editors. *The Chicago Manual of Style* and the NEHGS "house style" rules provided some direction, and the two prior guides published by NEHGS were very helpful. Readers may not agree with everything said in this guide, but all should find the contents to be useful for their genealogical writing, research, and knowledge.

Good genealogical writing in the United States evolved during the twentieth century from the use of implied or little documentation to the requirement of references to reliable sources for every statement of fact that is not public knowledge. Even in the past decade, the style of most genealogical journals changed from imbedded references to footnotes. In the twenty-first century, further changes will occur, no doubt. But good genealogical writing and scholarship will continue to build on the past, making guides like this a helpful contribution to the field.

Grateful thanks for the realization of this guide are due to Gabrielle Stone (Book Publications Supervisor), Carolyn Sheppard Oakley (Editor and Creative Director of *New England Ancestors*), and D. Brenton Simons (Assistant Executive Director) — and to the other authors: Lynn Betlock (Director of Marketing), Helen Schatvet Ullmann, CG (Associate Editor of the *Register*), Sharon DeBartolo Carmack, CG (genealogical author and editor), Michael J. Leclerc (Director of Electronic Publications), Rod Moody (Electronic Publications Editor), and Christopher Hartman (Director of Book Publications/Newbury Street Press).

Special thanks are due to Elizabeth Shown Mills, CG, CGL, FASG, whose many thoughtful comments and suggestions improved the text greatly. I also wish to thank other genealogical colleagues who reviewed the text and made valuable comments: Joseph C. Anderson II, CG, FASG; Robert Charles Anderson, FASG; Scott Andrew Bartley; David L. Greene, CG, FASG; Eric G. Grundset, MLS; Gale Ion Harris, FASG; Roger D. Joslyn, CG, FASG; David W. Kruger; Helen F. M. Leary, CG, CGL, FASG; Anita A. Lustenberger, CG;

Marsha Hoffman Rising, CG, FASG; Gary Boyd Roberts; Clifford L. Stott, AG, CG, FASG; and Helen Schatvet Ullmann, CG.

Henry B. Hoff, CG, FASG
Editor of The New England
Historical and Genealogical Register
July 2002

INTRODUCTION

It is most appropriate that the New England Historic Genealogical Society (NEHGS) publish a guide to writing — not only because today NEHGS actively publishes books, CD-ROMs, online articles, a journal, and a magazine but because historically so much of American genealogical writing has been shaped and influenced by NEHGS. Since its founding in 1845, NEHGS has played a leading role in establishing genealogical guidelines and determining a genealogical writing style.

The New England Historic Genealogical Society began to set the standard for American genealogical writing in 1847 when the first issue of its quarterly journal, *The New England Historical and Genealogical Register*, was published. The founding members of NEHGS intended not only to preserve important genealogical documents and materials, but also to disseminate such information and make it widely available to NEHGS members. The *Register*, therefore, contained previously unpublished historical and genealogical material, including transcriptions of source material and short genealogies. Looking back, the merits of this undertaking appear obvious, but at the time, the outcome was far from certain. In 1870, Rev. Edmund F. Slafter, author of the Society's "Twenty-Fifth Anniversary Discourse," reflected that "[T]he position to be occupied by this quarterly journal was altogether a new one; like the Society itself it was entering upon an untried experiment. No publication had occupied the same field or undertaken the same work." The longevity of the *Register* is a testament of the success of the endeavor. Published continuously since its first issue, without a single omission, the *Register* is the oldest genealogical journal in the world.

In his 1870 "Discourse," Rev. Slafter also mused on the state of genealogical writing. Prior to the founding of the New England Historic Genealogical Society in 1845, Rev. Slafter claimed that "scarcely anything had been done in this department. A few rudimentary attempts had been made but they were hardly worthy of the appellation of family histories. Most of them were . . . little more than a collection of names, thrown confusedly together without order or system of arrangement." One of the great contributions of the New England Historic Genealogical Society to the genealogical field was the introduction of an "order and system of arrangement" that provided organization and clarity — in short, the system now known as "*Register* style."

First introduced in the January 1870 issue of the *Register*, the new style was applied to an article on the genealogy of the Sherman family. As editor Albert Harrison Hoyt explained in the "Notes and Queries" section, "[F]or the benefit of future contributors to the *Register*, and perhaps of those about to publish family-genealogies, we have arranged the *Sherman Genealogy*, a portion of which appears in this number of the *Register*, on a plan easily understood, and convenient for reference." In the July 1883 issue of the *Register*, John Ward Dean reported on the use of the "*Register* plan for genealogical records." "It has now been in use thirteen years and has given satisfaction. The Publishing Committee will continue to require genealogies intended for the *Register* to be arranged on this plan." Although modifications have been made to *Register* style over the years to account for changing tastes and technologies, it remains fundamentally the same. Today, over 135 years after its introduction, the principles of *Register* style underpin the genealogical writing of the twenty-first century.

Building upon the foundation of *The New England Historical and Genealogical Register* and *Register* style, the New England Historic Genealogical Society has continued to set standards in other areas of genealogical writing. In addition to the *Register*, NEHGS books, CD-ROMs, *New England Ancestors* magazine, and the *NewEnglandAncestors.org* website have all benefited from the application of clear rules of style to sound genealogical scholarship. The accumulated knowledge and experience of the contributors to this volume, all New England Historic Genealogical Society authors and editors, establish anew the importance of following sound guidelines for genealogical writing.

Lynn Betlock
Managing Editor
New England Ancestors *magazine*

ABOUT NEHGS

New England Historic Genealogical Society
www.NewEnglandAncestors.org
101 Newbury Street, Boston, Massachusetts 02116-3007
Tel: 617-536-5740 • Fax: 617-536-7307
Email: *nehgs@nehgs.org*

> *The New England Historic Genealogical Society advances genealogical scholarship and develops the capabilities of both new and experienced researchers of family history by collecting, preserving, interpreting, and communicating — in a variety of accessible formats — reliable genealogical data with emphasis on families and communities connected to New England, as well as New York, Quebec, Atlantic Canada, Ireland, and England.*

Founded in 1845, the New England Historic Genealogical Society is the oldest genealogical organization in the United States. With over 20,000 members, it is also the largest. NEHGS offers a wide variety of resources for those interested in pursuing their family histories.

The NEHGS research library in Boston offers a comprehensive collection of more than 200,000 books, periodicals, and microform materials, as well as an enormous collection of more than one million manuscripts. Its book holdings include nearly all published New England genealogies, local histories, and related periodicals. Its microtext collection, with more than 40,000 items, contains copies of the original town, probate, land, and vital records; city directories; censuses; and immigration records for most of New England and eastern Canada. Beyond New England, family researchers will find many important published and primary sources for other regions, including New York, England, Ireland, Scotland, eastern Canada, French Canada, and continental Europe. NEHGS also provides a highly trained research staff, professional genealogists, and volunteers who are eager to help members and patrons in their research.

The Society also conducts a range of educational programs, from introductory lectures to extensive research tours. Other member benefits include:

- Online access to the NEHGS website, *www.NewEnglandAncestors.org*, which includes thousands of databases with millions of names.
- Unlimited onsite use of the NEHGS research library.
- Subscriptions to *New England Ancestors* and *The New England Historical and Genealogical Register*.
- Access to our reasonably priced Research Services when you need help.
- Access to our popular Online Genealogist for advice on research problems.
- Advance notice of, and discounts on, research services, tours and educational programs, and selected NEHGS books and CD-ROMs.

For more information about NEHGS,
visit *www.NewEnglandAncestors.org*
or call toll-free 1-888-296-3447.

ABOUT THE AUTHORS

LYNN BETLOCK is managing editor of *New England Ancestors* magazine and has written a number of articles for that publication.

SHARON DEBARTOLO CARMACK, CG, specializes in consulting, writing, and editing narrative family histories, as well as Irish and Irish-American family history research. She is the author of sixteen books and hundreds of articles and columns that have appeared in nearly every major genealogical journal and publication. Sharon is a partner in the research firm of Warren, Carmack & Associates.

PATRICIA LAW HATCHER, FASG, is a professional genealogist specializing in problem solving whose articles have appeared in over a dozen publications. She is the author of *Producing a Quality Family History* and is the editor of *The Pennsylvania Genealogical Magazine* and *The New York Genealogical and Biographical Record.* She is currently writing a forthcoming series of books on Colonial American research.

HENRY B. HOFF, CG, FASG, is editor of *The New England Historical and Genealogical Register.* He is the author of many genealogical articles and the compiler, editor, or co-editor of several books. He is a contributing editor of *The American Genealogist,* and for fifteen years he was editor or consulting editor of *The New York Genealogical and Biographical Record.*

MICHAEL J. LECLERC is director of special projects at the New England Historic Genealogical Society. He is the author of numerous genealogical articles in many journals and magazines. A past board member of the Association of Professional Genealogists, he currently serves as vice-president of administration for the Federation of Genealogical Societies.

ROD MOODY is former electronic publications editor for *NewEnglandAncestors.org.* He is the author of numerous articles for the website as well as *New England Ancestors* magazine.

CAROLYN SHEPPARD OAKLEY is the editor and creative director of *New England Ancestors* magazine. In addition to designing and editing this NEHGS publication, she also designs products and marketing materials for NEHGS departments. Carolyn came to NEHGS, originally in the sales department, in January 1999 and took her current position in July 2000. She had previously been employed as director of education and volunteers at the New Canaan Historical Society.

ALVY RAY SMITH, PhD, is the co-founder of Pixar Animation Studios, first director of computer graphics at Lucasfilm, Ltd., and winner of two technical Academy Awards. His PhD is from Stanford University. He is currently a trustee of the New England Historic Genealogical Society.

GABRIELLE STONE is former director of publications for the New England Historic Genealogical Society.

HELEN SCHATVET ULLMANN, CG, FASG, is associate editor of *The New England Historical and Genealogical Register*, a consulting editor for the Newbury Street Press, librarian at an LDS Family History Center, and a trustee of the Board for Certification of Genealogists. She has published articles in various genealogical journals and several books.

CHAPTER ONE

Writing as You Research: A Problem-Solving Tool Your Family Will Appreciate

Patricia Law Hatcher[1]

Birthdays, anniversaries, and holidays are often marked by giving and sharing. I have a suggestion for a gift that also will benefit your research. Too many of us see publishing our family history as a "someday" project, to be undertaken when our research is "done." Consider, instead, publishing your family history in pieces—with each piece a gift to your family. When you are ready to undertake a full-fledged family history, these pieces become the building blocks for your final book.

Keep the gift book relatively small. Focus on a single surname or geographical family cluster. You could begin this gift series with a compilation of the most recent generations of your family.

One benefit of sharing your research in small pieces is that your family is more likely to read it. A four-hundred-page book can be intimidating. Although proudly displayed on bookshelves and coffee tables, such tomes often rest there unopened and unread. Because the gift book is focused and small, the information isn't too overwhelming for family members to absorb.

Don't "dumb down" the gift publication for your family. It should contain all the genealogical material that you would put into a

---

[1] This article originally appeared in *New England Ancestors* magazine in the Holiday 2002 issue, vol. 3, nos. 5–6, pp. 27–28, 37, and on *NewEnglandAncestors.org* on November 1, 2002.

compiled family history. Consider it a dress rehearsal for the big production. Show-biz people expect that problems will be uncovered during dress rehearsal, but they plan to get them fixed before opening night.

The process of expressing our findings in writing—including proper use of terms such as *probably, possibly, likely,* and *maybe*—is the most valuable tool we have in our research kits. Unfortunately, it is also the most neglected. Many family researchers don't feel comfortable writing a research report themselves, and by the time they are ready to write a book, the number of hidden problems can be immense.

Don't omit the documentation—if you do, you may be doing family members a disservice. Some of them may want to know how you found out about Great-Uncle Albert's military career or how you found the land that Great-Grandpa homesteaded. There is nothing wrong, however, with making your book more family-friendly. You can print your sources as endnotes rather than footnotes. Switching between one and the other requires just a few mouse-clicks in almost any word-processing or genealogy database program.

As you prepare the genealogical section, you will probably find inadequate citations, inconsistencies, and omitted information. Furthermore, because you are focusing your concentration on such a small portion of your findings—and because you are approaching it with a fresh eye—you will likely identify new paths to research.

However, don't postpone the gift for your family because of a few minor problems or unexplored research opportunities—remember, this effort is a dress rehearsal. Keep a "to do" list for further research. On the other hand, if you realize that there is a big hole in the information you received many years ago from another researcher, and that perhaps you aren't descended from that Revolutionary War general after all, then *stop*. It isn't ethical to publish the bad information, even if it is "just for my family." Choose another surname for the gift. You can work on resolving the problem family in time for next year.

Because you have prepared the book according to genealogical standards, you will find that the carefully presented genealogical material you prepared for the book is perfect for exchanging information with fellow researchers.

By systematically writing about your research in focused pieces, you are likely to gain great benefits. Regularly preparing gift books for family members might be a crutch to make yourself write as you research, but it's one with rewards for both you and your family.

It is quick, easy, flexible, and relatively inexpensive to prepare a few copies of this family gift book through the services of a chain office supply store or copy center. The service is rapid, and you can often pick up the final product in a few hours—an important consideration in a season crowded with myriad last-minute tasks.

Keep things simple and use an 8.5x11 format. This lets you choose a generous-sized print that will be easier for elderly eyes to read. If there are only thirty to forty pages, print the pages single-sided, but if the number of pages is large, you can print them double-sided. Many types of papers are available. Spend some time browsing the

paper shelves at the office supply store or studying the sample book at the copy center. For a nominal amount, you could pick a gray or beige paper to give the book a "noncomputer" look. Laser printer and copy paper comes in several weights. The most common weight is 20 lb., but if you use white paper, you should choose 24 lb. for gift books. It feels substantial when the pages are turned, and there is less bleed-through from the next page, which also makes the text easier to read.

Copy centers offer a variety of binding styles. Visit those in your community and see what they have to offer. Spiral and plastic comb bindings are not a good idea for books donated to libraries, but they are great for family gift books because they lie open on a table or lap. Some copy centers have arrangements with outside vendors for hardbound books, but find out what the time requirement is for this service to make sure your schedule can accommodate it.

Color reproductions of photographs can be prohibitively expensive in a published book. On the other hand, the inclusion of a few color laser photocopies in each of the family gifts can be well worth the additional cost. Also consider photocopying (in color or black and white) other small items, such as graduation announcements, funeral cards, newspaper clippings, and so on.

Think about the mechanics of producing the book. There are many options. If you are doing only two or three copies, you could print all the pages yourself, copy the photographs yourself on the color laser copier at the copy center, and then have the stacks of paper bound. (*Hint*: Put a sheet of brightly colored paper between each volume to help keep them organized.) If you are printing a dozen or more copies or want double-sided pages, it is usually easier to have the copy center print them.

The per-book cost of these gift books may be much higher than printing hundreds of books through a commercial book printer, but the total out-of-pocket cost is very reasonable, especially if you are considering the books as part of your family gift-giving budget. The cost could run anywhere from $2 to $20, depending on your choices for reproduction, color copies, and binding.

Customize the contents. You can include information in gift books for your immediate family that you would not wish to share with the broader genealogical world, such as vital data about living persons. Stories that are fond memories for the family aren't nearly as interesting to readers who don't know the parties involved—and some of those stories could be embarrassing to the individuals involved if they were shared outside the family. They can be shared in the gift book and removed from the later genealogical publication.

If you are dealing with an ancestral family very far back in time, you can help your family understand how the people in the book relate to them by including charts. For a single surname, include a drop-line chart down to a family member they would know, such as a grandparent or great-grandparent. If you are presenting a geographical cluster, a focused pedigree chart would be helpful.

If you prepare all the pages yourself and use a copy center only for binding, you can even personalize each book for the individual recipient, adding a page saying "A gift from *me* to *you* on the occasion of *event*, given on *date*." If you have prepared the charts mentioned above, they can extend down to the individual recipient of the book.

If you will be giving the books to your family in person, you have the opportunity to share even more. Take along photographs, maps, and souvenirs from your research trip to the area where your ancestors lived. Add copies of the documents you found in your research. The family will be especially interested in those with signatures. The 1840 census may be familiar to us, but not to someone who hasn't been bitten by the genealogy bug. The deed with almost indecipherable handwriting that you used to identify the wife's name will be the perfect answer to "but it's so easy, isn't it, with everything on the Internet?"

You may benefit during this show-and-tell when a family member casually mentions a photograph, painting, letter, schoolbook, sampler, or other item he or she possesses. It seems that no matter how carefully we structure our genealogical interviews or query letters, our families seem to filter our questions through their understanding of what they think we need for our research. "Well, I didn't think you'd be interested in that" is an all-too-common comment. This sharing process may lead to invaluable new information.

PLAN FOR FAMILY GIFT BOOK

Recipients

I will give this book to: [list all names]

I will give this book on: [date]

Content

Title of book: [title]

This book will include: [list all family groups]

Illustrations: [list all, identify those in color]

Charts: [list dropcharts and pedigrees]

Will there be personalized pages? [describe]

Production

Number of pages: [number, single/double sided]

Type of paper: [weight, color, where to obtain]

Binding: [describe binding, including color]

Copy center to be used: [name]

Total books to print: [remember to keep a copy for yourself, and a couple of extras just in case]

Cost estimate: [total and per book]

CHAPTER TWO

Writing for *The New England Historical and Genealogical Register* and Other Genealogical Journals

Henry B. Hoff and Helen Schatvet Ullmann

Why do people write articles for *The New England Historical and Genealogical Register* and other genealogical journals? It requires a lot of work, it doesn't pay, and there's the indignity of the editing process during which your carefully constructed article is altered and rearranged. Nevertheless, the *Register* editors receive an average of one new article each week, almost all of which are unsolicited.

Authors have the satisfaction of knowing that their work is preserved and will be of use to researchers in the distant future. Many authors claim that they've sharpened their thinking from the writing process and learned from the editing process. Also, an article can be the best form of query. Experienced authors may publish one or more articles before publishing a full-scale genealogy in order to bring in new information and to publicize the project.

All genealogical journals are looking for new authors. If you see the same authors published again and again in journals, it is probably because they submit articles the editors want, in a form that approximates the journal's style, and they don't need extensive editing.

CONTENT

The *Register* editors are looking for articles on New England subjects or at least with a New England connection. Articles in the

Register often fall into one of the following four categories:

- Compiled accounts of families
- Problem-solving articles with a brief compiled account
- Immigrant origins with a brief compiled account
- Source material

Nevertheless, the *Register* has published numerous articles that don't fit any of these categories.

In the first three categories, articles usually begin with one or more paragraphs setting out (1) the problem(s), (2) what the author intends to accomplish, and (3) the author's familiarity with previous research on the subject and how the author's contribution fits with what is already known.[1] The author may then present relevant data and analysis, reach conclusions, and finally assemble the results in a brief compiled account (or genealogical summary). A summary of the principal methodology used or type of sources relied upon is desirable, if possible.

In his *Burnap-Burnett Genealogy*, Henry Wyckoff Belknap confused two men named Thomas Burnap who lived in Reading, Massachusetts, in the late 1600s. . . . Although Belknap correctly quoted a number of early Massachusetts records, he confused the probate records of the two Thomases who died two months apart in 1691. As a result he incorrectly concluded that Thomas, son of John, was the husband of Mary Pearson, and the father of her children. This in turn forced him to conclude that the Mary who was the wife of Thomas, son of Robert, was unidentified. He had, without realizing it, married the cousins to the same woman.

From George H. Perbix, "Thomas Burnap, Husband of Mary Pearson," Register 155 (October 2001):353-56 at 353

Articles usually begin with one or more paragraphs setting out the problem.

---

[1] Margaret F. Costello and Jane Fletcher Fiske, *Guidelines for Genealogical Writing: Style Guide for* The New England Historical and Genealogical Register *with Suggestions for Genealogical Books* (Boston: NEHGS, 1990), 1–2.

ACCOUNT BOOK AND FAMILY RECORD OF
ROBERT COOK OF NEEDHAM, MASSACHUSETTS

Transcribed by Timothy G. X. Salls

The following records were transcribed from a small (15.5 x 10 cm.), unpaginated, account book recently acquired by the R. Stanton Avery Special Collections Department of NEHGS from a rare book dealer in Pennsylvania. The provenance of this manuscript prior to its acquisition from the dealer is unknown.

The account book originally belonged to Robert Cook (1670–1756) of Needham, Massachusetts. He was born in Boston on 9 December 1670, son of Robert and Sarah (_____) Cook.[1] Robert Cook and Submit Weekes, both of Dorchester, were married on 26 October 1693 at the First Church in Boston.[2] Their first five children were born and baptized in Dorchester.[3] In 1701 or 1702 Robert Cook and his family moved to that part of Dedham that was set off as Needham in 1711.[4] He was active in town government, serving for many years as selectman, treasurer and assessor.[5] Submit (Weekes) Cook died in Needham 18 June 1748, and Robert Cook died there 1 April 1756.[6]

This account book provides more complete information on the children of Robert and Submit (Weekes) Cook than can be gleaned from the vital and church records of Dorchester, Dedham and Needham, and from the account of the family in Bonniebelle Wright Cook, *The Ancestors of Samuel Cook* (Lima, Okla.: by the author, 1995), 6–7. It also provides an interesting account of what Robert Cook's daughters received at marriage.

---

[1] *Boston Births, Baptisms, Marriages, and Deaths, 1630–1699, [Ninth] Report of the Record Commissioners* (Boston: Rockwell and Churchill, 1883), 114. The account book mentions "sister Elizabeth Smith of Boston" in 1730, but there is no birth record in Boston for an Elizabeth, daughter of Robert Cook. Submit (Weekes) Cook had an older sister, Elizabeth Weekes, born in 1653; however, no marriage is shown for her in Winifred Lovering Holman, *The Ancestry of Colonel Harrington Stevens and His Wife, Frances Helen Miller*, 2 vols. (Concord, N.H.; privately printed, 1948–52), 1:275.

[2] *Boston Births, Baptisms, Marriages, and Deaths* [note 1], 209.

[3] *Dorchester Births, Marriages, and Deaths to the End of 1825, [Twenty-First] Report of the Record Commissioners* (Boston: Rockwell and Churchill, 1890), 38–39, 41, 43–44; William Blake Trask, *Records of the First Church at Dorchester in New England 1636–1734* (Boston: George H. Ellis, 1891), 207–11.

[4] George Kuhn Clarke, *History of Needham, Massachusetts 1711–1911* (Cambridge, Mass.: University Press, 1912), 18, 72. On 1 January 1700/1 the selectmen of Dedham consented to the purchase by Robert Cooke of Dorchester of forty acres of land "granted to William Nahaton neer the vper falls."

[5] *Ibid.*, 648, 658, 675.

[6] Robert Brand Hanson, *Vital Records of Needham, Massachusetts 1711–1845* (Camden, Me.: Picton Press, 1997), 162.

From Register *155 (October 2001):391-96 at 391. The provenance and present location of source material should be given. Annotations may increase its usefulness to readers.*

In the fourth category, each type of source material (church records, Bible records, tax lists, account books, etc.) calls for distinctive treatment. In each case, authors should include information on the provenance of the material and perhaps the original recorder as well as its present location and availability in other formats or media. In most cases the original material should not be reordered.

The most important aspect of an article is content. The content should be new. If a family's genealogy has not previously been compiled or published, then a full compilation may be warranted. If there is already a good account of the family in print, then an article should just focus on correcting mistakes or presenting new discoveries without repeating much of the reliable material.

While many genealogists write articles on a single line of descent from an immigrant or other early ancestor, the *Register*'s policy is to publish balanced compiled accounts, that is, all descendants of an individual for perhaps two, three, or four generations, or at least all descendants bearing the same surname. Often some part of such a single-line article solves a particularly interesting problem and can stand alone as an article. The whole work could then be made available to the general public in some other medium, such as *NewEnglandAncestors.org*.

THE PROCESS

Submitting Articles to the *Register*

Since the *Register* is published using Microsoft® WORD, it is best to write your article in a recent version of WORD, if possible, and submit it as an email attachment or on a floppy disk with paper copy. Articles written in other programs and then converted to WORD often have serious formatting problems that are extremely time-consuming to resolve.

A template, "Write Your Family History in *Register* Style," can be downloaded from the Society's website at *www.NewEnglandAncestors .org/publications/register*. The template will enable you to utilize all the styles used in the *Register* using WORD. Accompanying text offers suggestions for shortcuts and footnotes as well as other useful tips.

However, you do not need to make your manuscript look like the final text. In the footnotes, do not refer to earlier footnotes, as their numbers very likely will be changed in the editing process. Give full publication information the first time a source is cited, and from then on, use a short title, or author's surname and short title. The editors will provide the necessary cross-references and alterations.

You may want to send the editors photocopies of relevant sources, especially original documents that are important to the article. If the article is source material, you should send photocopies of the originals.

While you might ask the editors whether they would be interested in a certain subject, please do not submit an article until you consider the research complete. The editors probably will ask questions that require further research; however, an article that is essentially finished is far more likely to be accepted and published fairly quickly than one that needs more research.

An article should be submitted to only one journal at a time. If the contents of an article have already appeared in print or will appear in print in some form, this should always be communicated to the editors so they are aware. Similarly, if you have previously worked on or published a related article, mention it.

Many authors email the editors in advance to let them know about their article or to ask questions. The current editor of the *Register* is Henry B. Hoff, and his email address is *nehgreditor@aol.com*; however, check the masthead page of the most recent *Register* to verify the current contact information. Helen Schatvet Ullmann is associate editor of the *Register*. It is always safe to send a paper copy of your article to: Editor of the *Register*, NEHGS, 101 Newbury Street, Boston, MA 02116-3007.

Acceptance

The editors' first priority is to produce each issue on time. Due to the high number of articles received, the editors cannot correspond extensively regarding new or potential articles. Most articles need substantial editing, and the editors can deal with only a limited number of articles at a time. Moreover, most articles are sent to one or more consulting editors for evaluation, adding to the time involved.

Once editing begins, the author will receive a permission letter to sign and return. This letter sets out the rights and responsibilities of

Only a certain number of articles can be accepted. The Register *publishes fewer than thirty articles a year.*

both NEHGS and an author. Articles that appear in the *Register* are archived on *NewEnglandAncestors.org* and are accessible to members only.

Only a certain number of articles can be accepted. Thus the editors have to choose those they feel are best suited for the *Register*. Sometimes the topic has already been treated in a recent or forthcoming article in the *Register* or another journal. At other times the style of the article is too informal for the *Register* but may be acceptable for another genealogical journal. An article may also hinge on an identification that the editors feel is too tentative to publish.

Frequently the editors decide that an article requires major editing, rewriting, and further research to make it ready for publication. They may not want to make a decision about the article until they have time to consider it.

In your cover letter you may want to ask the editors to recommend another journal in case your article is not right for the *Register* or if you want your article to be published sooner than the *Register*'s schedule permits. New England is fortunate in that there are many state and local genealogical journals publishing articles that are just as good as articles in the *Register*. Indeed, the *Register* editors have had many of their own articles published in state and local journals.

Another possible avenue of publication is *NewEnglandAncestors. org*. This is especially appropriate for very long articles and for articles on subjects that may not meet the current needs of the *Register*.

The Editing Process
Once the editors have accepted your article, editing may not begin for some time. During this period don't hesitate to email and ask when the editing process may begin. Once the editing process does begin, the editors will have questions that may require you to look at your files or conduct further research. If you will be traveling for any length of time, tell the editors in advance to help prevent delays while you are away.

The editing process usually takes months, with multiple drafts of the articles being emailed back and forth for questions and revisions.

Normally, authors will see the final version before publication; however, circumstances sometimes require the editors to make minor changes to an article at the last minute and there is not time to discuss those changes with the author.

Do not expand your article or change it drastically during the editing process. If you find something important (either positive or negative) during this period, discuss it immediately with the editors. What may appear to be a disaster at first glance may result in a better-focused article.

While it is almost impossible not to make a few mistakes, careful genealogists will "fact-check" their work before it is published. Going back over your semifinal draft to check *everything* against your notes and photocopies is tedious work—but it can be very rewarding. Not only will you catch possible typos or errors in page numbers or dates, you will also probably change the wording or even your reasoning. And you may make some new discoveries in the process! Nevertheless, for those errors that do get into print, the *Register* publishes additions and corrections in each October issue.

STYLE

General Comments

Each statement of fact that is not common knowledge should be cited to one or more reliable sources. This citation may not necessarily be to a primary source since a reliable secondary source sometimes is more appropriate. When an underlying original source is readily available, it should be consulted instead of relying on a published abstract. This is especially true when the related statement is crucial to your argument. Resources like Torrey's *New England Marriages Prior to 1700* or the *International Genealogical Index*, which were intended to be finding aids, should not be cited as sources. Find the original book, article, or document cited, examine it, and then include that original as your source.

An article should flow logically from one paragraph to the next. Thus a chronological approach may not be best (or even possible) for the entire article. Think carefully about how you are presenting

[16] Case of Wm. Graves Jan. 30 – Feb. 4, 1666/7, at pp. 23-30 of transcripts of "Depositions on Cases of Witchcraft Tried in Connecticut, 1662-1693," in the Samuel Wyllys Papers, Brown University Library, Providence, R.I. (and published here with the permission of the Library). A microfilm of photostatic copies of the original depositions is in the Connecticut State Library but it is barely legible. The depositions from this case were published in David D. Hall, *Witch-Hunting in Seventeenth-Century New England: A Documentary History, 1638-1692* (Boston: Northeastern University Press, 1991), 164–69.

From Norbert R. Bankert, "More on the Identity of Abigail (Graves) Dibble, and Her Tragic Death and Suspicions of Witchcraft," Register 155 (July 2001):273-78 at 275

The original documents examined are cited. Since they have been published, this citation must also be given.

the material. What may be clear to you after working with the family for years may bewilder a reader. A simple chart may clarify complex relationships. When submitting a draft article, you may want to write a few comments to the editors in bold within brackets.

In a cover letter, you may want to inform the editors of relevant sources you reviewed but did not cite (for example, an undocumented website). If your article does not mention a relevant source, especially one contrary to your position, the editors and readers may assume that you had failed to find it.

Avoid "bootstrapping," that is, as the argument is being developed in the article, the author refers to an identification as if it were already proved—when it hasn't been yet.

Besides citing sources, footnotes can convey much other useful information. If a footnote contains more than one source, it may be helpful to indicate which source supports which fact. Footnotes might include an evaluation of a source, a parenthetical remark, or a point that digresses from the flow of the text and yet is important to make. While an article often corrects earlier material in print or manuscript, it may not be necessary to say so in the text. However, the author will want the reader to know that he or she is aware of the conflict, where the outdated or erroneous material has appeared, and perhaps the argument for the correction.

"I" and "we" should be used sparingly in articles. The *Register* editors do not accept a "travelogue" style, that is, a description of the research process, but this style can make for interesting reading and other editors may accept it.

See chapter 6 of this book, "Writing and Style." More detailed advice may be found in works by Patricia Law Hatcher and Elizabeth Shown Mills.[2]

Register Style

The term "*Register* style" refers to the way in which the editors of the *Register* have presented vital and biographical data on families since 1870. The most important points will be presented here and in the illustrations. For variations and nuances, see current issues of the *Register*. Two prior guides published by NEHGS give further details.[3]

While *Register* style may take some getting used to, it provides readers with a standard template for articles, rather than each author's own invented approach. In addition, authors generally find it easier to have a template when writing articles.

The basic unit for presenting in *Register* style is the family group. The earliest head of a family group is assigned the number 1. Following the given name, a superscripted number informs the reader how many generations from the immigrant this person is removed. His or her name is followed by a "lineage line" in italics, giving the name of each

---

[2] Patricia Law Hatcher, *Producing a Quality Family History* (Salt Lake City: Ancestry, 1996); Elizabeth Shown Mills, *Evidence! Citation & Analysis for the Family Historian* (Baltimore: Genealogical Publishing Co., 1997); Elizabeth Shown Mills, ed., *Professional Genealogy: A Manual for Researchers, Writers, Editors, Lecturers, and Librarians* (Baltimore: Genealogical Publishing Co., 2001).

[3] Costello and Fiske, *Guidelines for Genealogical Writing* [see note 1]; Thomas Kozachek, *Guidelines for Authors of Compiled Genealogies* (Boston: Newbury Street Press, 1998).

A sample paragraph for a head of a family group

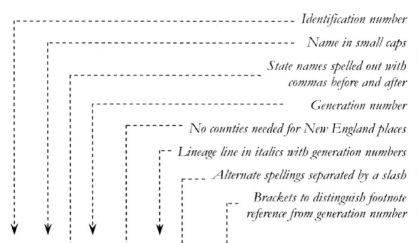

Identification number

Name in small caps

State names spelled out with commas before and after

Generation number

No counties needed for New England places

Lineage line in italics with generation numbers

Alternate spellings separated by a slash

Brackets to distinguish footnote reference from generation number

5. WILLIAM³ MILLS (*Benjamin²*, *Samuel¹*), was born at Dedham, Massachusetts, on 2 May 1682,[1] and he died at Needham, Massachusetts, on 9 July 1759.[2] He married first on 28 May 1714, MARY WARE, born on 6 April 1691, daughter of Ebenezer and Martha (Herring) War.[3] Given the birth of her last child and the date of William's remarriage, she must have died in 1722 or 1723. William was of Needham when he married second, at the Second Church in Roxbury, Massachusetts, on 17 June 1724, MARY (MOREY) WATSON,[4] widow of Charles Watson, having married him at Roxbury, Massachusetts, on 2 March 1714/15.[5] She was born at Roxbury on 11 August 1682, daughter of Thomas and Susanna (Newell) Mowrey/Morey.[6] She was the "Widow of William Mills Senr" who died at Needham on 3 October 1759.[7]

Note that places generally precede dates of events and that abbreviations are not used. Note also that each piece of information has a corresponding footnote. A date before 1752 and between 1 January and 24 March should be expressed as a double-date (e.g., 2 March 1714/5), or as 2 March 1714[/5] if inferred from the context, or as 2 March 1714[/5?] if uncertain.

progenitor back to the immigrant—and sometimes earlier if the information is known.[4]

For example, an article on Mary Braddock, a fourth-generation New Englander, might initially identify her as:

> 1. MARY[4] BRADDOCK (*Nathaniel[3], Robert[2], William[1]*), OR
> 1. MARY[4] BRADDOCK, daughter of Nathaniel[3] (*Robert[2], William[1]*) and Susan (Taylor) Braddock

The account of Mary Braddock that followed would be considered *text*—while the account of her children would be *subtext*. As will be seen in the illustrations, abbreviations and an abbreviated style are used in subtext.

After Mary Braddock's name and lineage line or parentage would come her place of birth and date of birth, assuming they are known. If there is a question about place of birth, it may be preferable to put the date of birth first. So, for example:

> Born at Marlborough, Massachusetts, about 1718, OR
> Born about 1718, probably at Marlborough, Massachusetts

Her place and date of death and burial may come next or may be towards the end of the text, depending on circumstances. For example, if Mary Braddock outlived three husbands and evidence of her date and place of death requires discussion, towards the end of the text is probably a better place. Frequently an exact date of death is not known and a statement like the following is appropriate:

> Died between 2 July 1772 (date of will) and 3 September 1772 (probate of will)

Usually statements should be footnoted the first time they are made; however, there will be instances like "date of will" or "probate of will" when it is evident the citation will be given later in the text.

---

[4] Superscript style for pre-American ancestry differs; see current issues of the *Register* for examples.

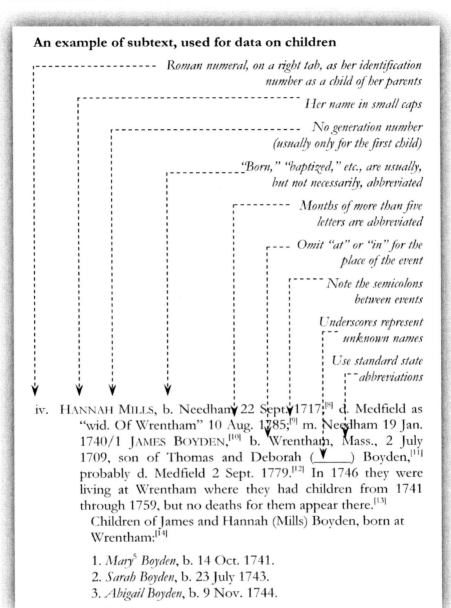

An example of subtext, used for data on children

Roman numeral, on a right tab, as her identification number as a child of her parents

Her name in small caps

No generation number (usually only for the first child)

"Born," "baptized," etc., are usually, but not necessarily, abbreviated

Months of more than five letters are abbreviated

Omit "at" or "in" for the place of the event

Note the semicolons between events

Underscores represent unknown names

Use standard state abbreviations

iv. HANNAH MILLS, b. Needham 22 Sept. 1717;[8] d. Medfield as "wid. Of Wrentham" 10 Aug. 1785;[9] m. Needham 19 Jan. 1740/1 JAMES BOYDEN,[10] b. Wrentham, Mass., 2 July 1709, son of Thomas and Deborah (_____) Boyden,[11] probably d. Medfield 2 Sept. 1779.[12] In 1746 they were living at Wrentham where they had children from 1741 through 1759, but no deaths for them appear there.[13]

Children of James and Hannah (Mills) Boyden, born at Wrentham:[14]

1. *Mary*[5] *Boyden*, b. 14 Oct. 1741.
2. *Sarah Boyden*, b. 23 July 1743.
3. *Abigail Boyden*, b. 9 Nov. 1744.

Note that commas rather than semicolons separate events (birth and death) for the spouse. Including the surname for each child makes an electronic search feasible. If biographical information on a child is extensive, it may be better to also make him or her the head of a separate family group.

Place and date of marriage should follow, with an indication of first or later marriage. For example:

> Married first, at the Bozrah Congregational Church, Norwich, Connecticut, on 28 April 1740, WILLIAM EDGERTON.

Only partial information may be available, and again you want to indicate why you are making each statement. For example:

> Married before 12 February 1742 (when their first child was baptized), perhaps at Norwich, Connecticut, where her parents were living.

The identification of the spouse follows his or her name, and it is usually in the same order as above. Continuing this example, the spouse might be:

> WILLIAM EDGERTON, born at Norwich on 20 April 1715, died before 2 January 1765 (when his wife remarried), son of Richard and Lucy (Smith) Edgerton.

Parents of spouses should be mentioned as it makes the article more complete and useful to more readers.

After these one or two paragraphs, biographical information on the couple follows, usually in chronological order. Finally their children are listed in subtext. Illustrations show the conventional order of data, punctuation, and abbreviations typical of *Register* style. Each child has a lower-case Roman numeral, and any child carried forward is given an Arabic numeral, following from the number assigned to the last child carried forward in the previous family group.[5]

---

[5] The "Modified *Register*" style (or system) assigns an Arabic numeral to all children in a family, and indicates those carried forward by a plus sign. This is the system currently used by *National Genealogical Society Quarterly*. For further information and discussion about nuances of use, see Joan Ferris Curran, Madilyn Coen Crane, and John H. Wray, *Numbering Your Genealogy: Basic Systems, Complex Families, and International Kin*, National Genealogical Society Special Publication No. 64 (Arlington, Va.: National Genealogical Society, 2000).

Grandchildren may be listed here, depending on the scope of the article.

Be consistent in your overall style, even if not conforming to *Register* style in all respects. Some authors make their own check-lists for overall style and completeness.

Authors should be aware that genealogy computer programs claiming to generate a *"Register-style report"* are usually quite deficient. Such a report, if used, will need substantial editing by the author prior to submission in WORD.

OTHER JOURNALS

Other American genealogical journals have comparable styles. It is best to write an article with a specific journal in mind. Even if you end up giving your article to a different journal, the editor should be able to convert it to the style of that journal, as long as you have been consistent.

Checklist for "Writing for *The New England Historical and Genealogical Register* and Other Genealogical Journals"

☑ Does the content of your article fit with *Register* preferences?

☑ Is the content of your article new?

☑ Are you using WORD?

☑ Is your research complete?

☑ Are your footnotes complete?

☑ Is each statement of fact that is not common knowledge cited to one or more reliable sources?

☑ Does your article flow logically from one paragraph to the next?

☑ Does your article include material that should be moved from text to footnotes—or omitted entirely?

☑ Does your article conform to *Register* style?

☑ Have you been consistent in your overall style?

CHAPTER THREE

Writing for *New England Ancestors* and Other Popular Genealogical Magazines

Sharon DeBartolo Carmack

There's no better time to be a genealogical writer. With many magazines that publish articles for a popular audience and others geared for professional genealogists, you can pick and choose where you'd like to see your byline. Maybe you'll want to see your work appear in all of them. While all these publications have the goal of reaching the beginning genealogist as well as the established researcher, few people subscribe to or read all of them. That means each publication reaches a slightly different audience. But all of these magazines need good writers who know how to meet deadlines, and several of them will pay you for your submission. So how do you break into the popular genealogical writing market? It's really not that difficult to go from article idea to bylined author.

YOUR ARTICLE IDEAS

I'll never forget the first time I chatted with Elizabeth Shown Mills, CG, FASG, then editor of the *National Genealogical Society Quarterly*, when I became editor of the *Association of Professional Genealogists Quarterly*. We were talking about article ideas. She said, "Coming up with ideas is easy. It's finding good, qualified writers to write them." Elizabeth didn't know it at the time, but I was inwardly shaking, thinking I would surely run out of ideas by the second or third issue. That was in 1989, and she was right: in more than seventeen years as a writer and editor, I've had to come up with ideas not only for articles I wanted to write but also ideas for articles to suggest to writers. So far, the well hasn't gone dry.

One of the best ways to get ideas for articles is to read or scan all the popular magazines and attend national conferences. You'll notice that there are only a few core topics in genealogy and most of them revolve around types of sources, methods for using sources, and research/problem-solving techniques. So what could be left for you to write about? Hasn't everything been covered already? To a degree, yes, but each person can bring a new spin to a core topic. Many people have written on or lectured about the census, for example, but each writer approaches the topic a bit differently. One might deal with the basics of census research, another might cover the use of pre-1850 censuses, another might focus on correlating census data through the decades, and yet another might address using censuses online. Your job is to find an approach that someone hasn't used yet, or that you use differently.

After you establish yourself with a magazine and an editor, don't hesitate to ask that editor for ideas he or she would like to see covered. In fact, editors often have ideas for articles and then look for people to write them. Let your editor know of your willingness to research and write on a variety of topics and ask to be kept in mind for assignments.

FINDING THE RIGHT MARKET FOR YOUR ARTICLE

Once you have an idea for an article, the next step will be to decide which magazine your article is best suited for. Almost all popular genealogical magazines offer writer's guidelines. Request them and study the types of articles in each of the magazines. Who are the magazine's readers? *New England Ancestors*, for example, goes to all members of the New England Historic Genealogical Society and, therefore, reaches people who are serious about genealogy, from the beginner to the advanced researcher. On the other hand, the majority of *Family Tree Magazine* readers are beginners in genealogy, so articles are written with that audience in mind. Those who subscribe to the Federation of Genealogical Societies (FGS) *FORUM* presumably have an intermediate to advanced research skill level.

Along with the level of genealogist each magazine reaches, also note the types of articles the magazine publishes. *Family Tree Magazine* does not publish case studies; it focuses on how-to articles. The FGS *FORUM* gears many of its articles and columns to the needs of genealogical society members and officers. Readers of the *Association of Professional Genealogists Quarterly* are not only genealogists who take clients but also librarians, instructors, heir tracers, and genealogical book vendors. *Ancestry* publishes how-to articles, "light" case studies, and human-interest stories, as do *Family Chronicle* and Everton's *Genealogical Helper*. *Internet Genealogy* caters to "technogenealogists." *New England Ancestors* prefers articles that focus on the New England region, but it also publishes general articles covering all parts of the country.

Popular genealogical magazine editors want articles written in a conversational tone, as I've written this chapter. That is, address your reader as "you," find a good "hook" for the opening paragraph that will draw in the reader, add some appropriate humor, use contractions, end sentences with prepositions as you would in conversation, and avoid the passive voice.

Be careful of how much you insert yourself into the article. While there is nothing wrong with telling the reader how you did something, readers are more interested in how *they* can do something. This chapter is a perfect example. I could have written it on how I've been published in popular genealogical magazines, since it's based on my experiences as a popular writer and editor, but who really cares? You want to know how you can get published in popular genealogical magazines. So the chapter is you-focused, not I-focused.

GOING RATES FOR MAGAZINE ARTICLES

If you are supplementing your genealogical income as a writer, then part of deciding where to send an article may be based on what different magazines pay. You can earn from zero to $800 for an article. Only one magazine pays upon acceptance of the article; all of the others pay upon publication, which means you may not see a paycheck for several months if the article isn't published right away.

But don't let writers' fees cloud your vision if your goal is to write, get published, and make a name for yourself in genealogy. The field of genealogy, while it has become more commercialized, still relies heavily on its volunteer force. If you can't volunteer in the organizations you belong to because you are homebound or have a full-time job, then consider writing for the society's publication as your contribution. Sometimes just the prestige of being published in a highly respected magazine, such as *New England Ancestors*, is as valuable as receiving monetary remuneration. In addition, you'll be adding to your bibliography.

QUERYING THE EDITOR

Most genealogical editors prefer that you send them a "query" rather than a completed manuscript of an article. This means you pitch your article idea in a letter or email, asking if the editor would be interested in having you write the article. There is no need to spend your time and energy writing an article that no magazine is interested in. It's a much softer blow to your writer's ego to have an idea, and not a completed article, rejected.

Keep your query short and to the point. A good query is no longer than a hard-copy page. Your letter should do the following:

- Address the editor by name. "To Whom It May Concern" is also acceptable, but do not use "Dear Sir."
- Grab the editor's attention in the opening paragraph as you would in the first paragraph of an article.
- Clearly state your article idea (or an outline) and the direction of the article: what the article is about, what your slant is, why this is a hot topic, how many words you envision the article will be, and what illustrations you suggest.
- State why you are the best person to write this article (give your qualifications).
- Tell when you can deliver the article.

Always double-check your query letter or email for errors and typos, and if using regular mail, include a self-addressed, stamped envelope. Some editors will respond within a week; others may take several months to respond.

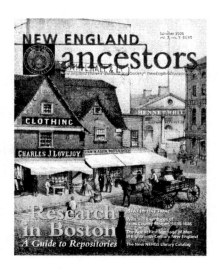

Can you send simultaneous queries to multiple editors? In other words, can you send the same query or completed manuscript to more than one editor at the same time? While some editors don't mind this and ask only that you make them aware that this is a simultaneous submission in your cover letter, others frown upon the practice.

Assuming the editor likes your article idea, he or she may offer you a boilerplate contract or publishing agreement for you to sign. There are many good books that explain rights and publishing contracts, such as Brad Bunnin and Peter Beren's *The Writer's Legal Companion* (New York: Perseus Books, 1999). See also my book, *Carmack's Guide to Copyright and Contracts: A Primer for Genealogists, Writers & Researchers* (Baltimore: Genealogical Publishing Company, 2005). A good rule, however, is not to sign anything you don't understand.

RESEARCHING AND WRITING THE ARTICLE

Mystery writer Sandra Brown said, "The worst piece of advice I was ever given was to write about what I know. I took stock of what I knew and, from a creative standpoint, none of it was very stimulating. . . . I have no personal knowledge of, or experience with, paramilitary hate groups, or heart transplantation, or escapees from maximum security prisons, or what it's like to be profoundly deaf. But I've written about all these topics, and the books became best sellers." While we may not be writing mystery bestsellers, we can apply Brown's quote to genealogical writing, too. Genealogists by their nature are researchers. If you are assigned a topic or just have an interest in a topic, research it well enough to write a popular article about it. As part of your research, you should interview colleagues who know more than you do about the topic so you can quote them as experts in your article.

The more you write, the easier (and quicker) it will become to research and write articles. And the more you write, the better you will become at judging how long it will take you to research and write an article. You will find it helpful to outline your article, either on paper or mentally, before you begin writing. This outline will help guide your research.

As you study the genealogical magazines, you'll notice some of the same writers' names cropping up. How do they write so many articles? They have learned to write fast. David Fryxell's *How to Write Fast (While Writing Well): A Guide to Speed, Organization, Concentration, Problem-Solving, and Creativity* (Cincinnati: Writer's Digest Books, 1992) is an excellent resource if you want to do a lot of writing for popular genealogical magazines. This book will give you advice on how to juggle multiple writing projects and show you how to get the most information out of the research you need to write on a topic for a popular genealogical magazine.

As you are writing the article, stay conscious of the word count. The word limit the editor gives you in your contract is there for a reason. The editor knows exactly how much space 3,000 words takes up in the magazine. Significantly going over or under the limit won't endear you to an editor.

Keep your audience in mind, too, as you write. Articles for popular genealogical magazines are meant to inform and instruct. Don't forget to include basic information for the reader, such as mentioning a website *and* its URL, giving an acronym *and* spelling it out at the first mention, referencing a book *and* including the publication information (city, publisher, and date).

THE DREADED "D" WORD

All magazines run on deadlines, and the editor will give you one when he or she sends you a contract. When you are discussing the article with the editor or negotiating the contract, if the deadline is unrealistic, don't be afraid to ask for a later date. Deadlines tend to creep up faster than you expect. Better to say something early on and ask for more time rather than miss the date.

To avoid missing your deadline, put the date in red on your calendar—but mark it for at least a week earlier than the deadline the editor gave you. That way you'll be early with your article, and your editor will love you. If the deadline is for the first of a month, always mark a due date in the previous month. You don't want to be caught by surprise when you flip your calendar page to a new month and discover you've got an article due on the first, and you haven't even begun thinking about it yet.

Missing a deadline has a snowball effect on everyone who works on the magazine. Sure, everyone misses a deadline now and then, but if it's more than a day or two late, or you are habitually late—even if you keep the editor apprised—your editor will probably start favoring other writers who make deadlines sacred dates. Those writers whose names you see regularly in popular genealogical magazines? They're always getting articles published because they always meet their deadlines.

SUBMITTING YOUR ARTICLE

The writer's guidelines for the magazine you're writing for should tell you the house style, how to format your manuscript, and how to submit it to the editor (on a computer disk with a paper copy or by email attachment). "House style" is how the magazine makes each article look consistent within the publication. For example, some magazines may spell out numbers one through ninety-nine, while others will only spell out numbers one through ten, then use numerals. Or one magazine might use the series comma (that is, a comma separating all elements in a series, such as red, white, and blue), while another may not use the series comma (red, white and blue). Some may use endnotes; others prefer references be within the text or as part of sidebars.

One pet peeve of many editors is the writer who formats the manuscript to match the publication's look. Most editors want old-fashioned-looking manuscripts even if you are submitting it electronically, that is, double-spaced, no columns, printed on one side of 8.5 x 11 paper, with one-inch margins all around. Don't use fancy fonts: Times New Roman 12 point is fine. Don't add graphics to the manuscript; send them as separate electronic files or print them out on separate pages.

After you submit your article, it will go through copyediting. This is where the editor or a copyeditor reads your article for flow and continuity, tightens sentences, fixes any grammatical problems, adjusts the article to house style, or possibly reorganizes the article. Maybe the third paragraph would work better as the first paragraph, or a section toward the end of the article flows better in the middle. Depending on your writing skill, how closely you've matched the style and voice of the magazine, and how light- or heavy-handed the editor is with the red pen, your article may look almost identical to the way you submitted it; it could also look as if it was rewritten. Don't be too alarmed. All articles get edited, even those written by experienced, professional writers. Writers are usually too close to their material to see how an article can be improved. Of utmost importance, however, is that the editor hasn't inadvertently changed the meaning of any of your sentences or your article. Unfortunately, not all magazines return the copyedited manuscript to the writer. This is something you need to ask about when you negotiate your contract. If you do get to see the copyedited manuscript, inform the editor if your meaning has been changed during copyediting.

After copyediting, the article is laid out as it will appear in the magazine. If you are given the opportunity to review at this stage, what you will see is called either "galleys" or "page proofs." If your contract does not stipulate an author review at this stage, ask the editor if you can review proofs. While the magazine will have proofreaders to check for typos and layout problems, it always makes an author feel more comfortable to see the article right before it goes to press. When the editor mails, faxes, or emails you the pages, review and return them with any corrections by the date the editor tells you. Keep in mind that at the page proof stage, you cannot make any major changes or additions. You may correct only typos or glaring errors. Adding even one sentence might affect the pagination and subsequently everything that follows your article.

BASKING IN THE BYLINE

Not long after you've reviewed the page proofs, you'll receive the actual magazine with your article published. Nothing can compare to that feeling of seeing your name in print for the first time—or the hundredth time. You'll carry around the issue everywhere you go and proudly show it to friends and family. But don't bask too long. You've got more articles to write!

Checklist for "Writing for *New England Ancestors* and Other Popular Genealogical Magazines"

- ☑ Survey and study the popular genealogical magazines.
- ☑ Pick topics that interest you, and then see how you can put a new spin on them.
- ☑ Review the popular magazines and decide where to pitch your article, based on your topic, circulation, pay, and prestige.
- ☑ Query the editor in one page, presenting your article idea, your qualifications, and your proposed delivery date.
- ☑ Once the magazine has accepted your article idea, begin researching and writing the article.
- ☑ Remember, the more you write, the better and quicker at it you'll become.
- ☑ Be a writer editors love: Stick to the word limit and submit your article by the deadline, early if possible.
- ☑ Submit the manuscript according to the magazine's writer's guidelines.
- ☑ Ask to review copy edits or page proofs, then do so in a timely manner.
- ☑ Proudly show off your published article, then begin the process all over again!

More Information on *New England Ancestors*
New England Historic Genealogical Society
101 Newbury Street
Boston, MA 02116-3007
Email: *magazine@nehgs.org*
Website: *www.NewEnglandAncestors.org*

New England Ancestors magazine offers a variety of features and columns, designed to appeal to a wide range of genealogical and historical interests. Articles highlight useful research sources, relate interesting historical episodes, offer instructive case studies, and much more. Appropriate for family historians of every level, this popular magazine is a benefit of NEHGS membership.

Frequency: Five times per year. *Circulation*: 20,000. *Rights*: Requires a signed agreement granting NEHGS the right to archive the text of the article in a members-only area of *www.NewEnglandAncestors.org*; permission to reprint and/or republish the article, as originally published in *New England Ancestors*, at any time and in any manner in keeping with the mission of NEHGS, including compilations and electronic format; and the author's agreement not to publish the article in any other journal or magazine, or by any electronic means, without first consulting the editors of *New England Ancestors* and citing *New England Ancestors*. *Average length of articles*: 1,200 to 2,750 words. Query or submit completed manuscript. Query by email. Response time to query: 1 to 2 months. Does not accept simultaneous submissions and rarely previously published submissions. Submit article electronically (disk or email attachment) and hard copy. Writer's guidelines available by mail or email.

CHAPTER FOUR

Writing for *NewEnglandAncestors.org* and Other Websites

Michael J. Leclerc and Rod Moody

As the Internet has matured over the past decade, so too have the conventions for writing for websites. As in any form of publishing, it is important to follow established norms to ensure that readers will be able to best understand your writing and utilize the important information contained therein.

The primary consideration when writing for any publication is to think about how the reader will approach and interpret the text. Style guidelines for grammar, punctuation, capitalization, names, dates, quotes, statistical presentations, etc., remain essentially the same for all NEHGS publications. Please refer to the chapters that illustrate style guidelines for our print publications for this information. This chapter will cover the differences between writing for the Internet and writing for print publications.

Writing for an online audience is similar to writing for a periodical. Most readers will scan until they find something that catches their eye. Most online readers are searching for information that is easy to locate, easy to digest, and easy to print. With this in mind, it is reasonable to try to present text in a way that will fulfill these criteria.

ARTICLE LENGTH

The amount of text that is displayed on a single page of a website is important. According to Nielson Netratings, 204 million Americans (75% of the entire population of the United States) uses the Internet. The Pew Internet & Family Life Project reports that only 39% of urban and suburban dwellers and 24% of rural Americans have broadband or digital subscriber line (DSL) high-speed access. If a lengthy article is displayed on a single web page, it could take a considerable amount of time to download that page for those without high-speed access. This delay defeats the main purposes of web content—ease of use and quick results. It is up to the editor to decide how to split lengthy articles into separate pages. Writers need to realize that long articles will be divided, and should plan their content accordingly. If there are no clear lines of division within the text, the editor may ask the author to rewrite the article. Authors tempted to "write long" should also keep in mind that the vast majority of web users will not read an article word for word. As previously noted, most readers of web content prefer to scan the page. The *maximum* length for any article posted on a single page of *NewEnglandAncestors.org* is 3,000 words. The average length is 2,000 words.

ENHANCEMENTS

When designing and formatting a web page, you can employ several techniques to attract the reader's attention. The most common are listed below.

Hyperlinks

Hyperlinks enable readers to go instantly to an area that interests them most with a click of a mouse. A hyperlink is created in HyperText Markup Language (HTML), which renders normal text into underlined "clickable" text. Hyperlinks are not limited to text. Images and icons can also serve as hyperlinks. Hyperlinks can be used to reference a different location on that page, another location with a website, or any other location on the Internet. Hyperlinks to email addresses are also commonly used. Maureen Taylor's article "Scoundrels in Rhode Island" (*NewEnglandAncestors.org*, November 9, 2001) shows how hyperlinks can help both the reader and the author:

> Civil and criminal court cases kept by the <u>Rhode Island Supreme Court Judicial Records Center</u> can be a gold mine for researchers. Their archives contain civil and criminal court cases (1671-1900), divorce cases (1749-1900), and

some naturalization papers (1793-1974). Online order forms are available on their website for specific requests, but for general information about the archives' holdings, send an <u>email request</u> to them. All court cases after 1900 must be requested via regular mail. See their website for further details.

In the above example, clicking on the first underlined text takes readers to the Judicial Records Center website, where they can download an online order form. Readers may also click on the underlined "email request" text, which will automatically launch the email program with the address already filled in. Notice also that the last sentence advises readers to see the website for further details, as there is far too much information to be included in the article.

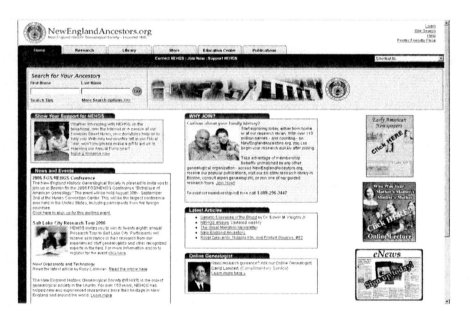

Another valuable use for hyperlinks is to jump to other pages within the same site. When writing for *NewEnglandAncestors.org*, think in terms of what hyperlinks you can provide that would be beneficial to the reader. For instance, in Patricia Law Hatcher's article, "Land Records: New England's Under-Appreciated Genealogical Source"

(*NewEnglandAncestors.org*, February 15, 2002), she urges readers to visit other areas of the NEHGS website for additional information by adding hyperlinks, as shown in the following example:

> Land records are also voluminous. The indexes alone might require many rolls of microfilm. On a recent NEHGS trip to the Family History Library in Salt Lake City, NEHGS Librarian David Dearborn and I agreed that, for this reason, focusing on land records is a highly efficient use of a researcher's time in Salt Lake City.
>
> *Tip*: Learn more about NEHGS Tours and Education events.
>
> In Connecticut, Rhode Island, and Vermont, deeds are maintained at the town level. In Maine, Massachusetts, and New Hampshire, they are at the county level, although original grants are at the town level.
>
> *Tip*: To learn more about the location of New England land records, see Marcia D. Melnyk's Genealogist's Handbook for New England Research.

In her first paragraph, Hatcher indicates that researching land records in Salt Lake City is a worthwhile endeavor. She then provides a link to the page where interested readers could sign up for an NEHGS research tour to Salt Lake City. Next, she writes about where the records are kept in various New England states and follows by adding a link to the NEHGS online bookstore, where the reader can buy books that explain New England research in greater detail.

Bulleted Lists and Tables

As the following example demonstrates, bulleted lists are an excellent way to attract a reader's attention while presenting the information in an easy-to-read format. Just imagine how the example, from Sherry L. Gould's "Genealogical Resources at New Hampshire State Archives" (*NewEnglandAncestors.org*, June 28, 2002), would look without the bullet points!

COURT RECORDS

The court records found at the Archives are an excellent source of information about the lives of the people of the state. Like the petitions, these are original records.

- Provincial Period (pg. 52) 1630s through 1772
- Hillsborough County (pg. 9) 1772 through the first decade of the 1900s, depending on the series
- Merrimack County (pg. 12) from its inception in 1823 through 1900
- Rockingham County (pg. 10) 1772 through 1920
- Strafford County (pg. 32) 1780 through 1899, which are not yet processed
- Sullivan County (pg. 35) from incorporation in 1827 through 1919
- Belknap County (pg. 10) 1840 through 1899
- Grafton County records (pg. 9) 1773 to 1899, partially indexed

Tables can divide complex information that is not easily readable as a paragraph into a format that makes sense to everyone. The following information is adapted from the introduction to *Vital Records of Marlborough, Massachusetts, to the Year 1850* (Worcester, Mass.: Franklin P. Rice, 1908):

MARLBOROUGH, MIDDLESEX COUNTY.

On May 31, 1660, a grant was made to the Whip-suffrage planters. The name of the plantation was "Marlborow." Additional lands, from a tract called "Agaganquamasset," were granted to Marlborough July 2, 1700, and Nov. 16, 1716. The section called "Chauncy" was set off as the new town of Westborough Nov. 18, 1717. A part was established at Southborough on July 6, 1727. A part was included in the District of Berlin on March 16, 1784. The towns of Westborough, Southborough, and Berlin are now part of Worcester County. A part of Framingham was annexed to

Marlborough on Feb. 23, 1791. A part of Marlborough was annexed to Northborough on June 20, 1807. A part was annexed to Bolton Feb. 11, 1829. A part of Southborough was annexed to Marlborough March 24, 1843.

Try looking at this information set off into a table and introduced by a subheading:

CHART 1 IMPORTANT DATES FOR MARLBOROUGH RESEARCHERS	
May 31, 1660	Marlborow plantation granted to Whip-suffrage planters.
July 2, 1700	Agaganquamasset lands annexed
November 16, 1716	Additional Agaganquamasset lands annexed
November 18, 1717	Chauncy section of Marlborough set off as the town of Westborough
July 6, 1727	Part of Marlborough set off as the town of Southborough
March 16, 1784	Section of Marlborough set off as part of the District of Berlin
February 23, 1791	Part of Framingham annexed to Marlborough
June 20, 1807	Part of Marlborough annexed to Northborough
February 11, 1829	Part of Marlborough annexed to Bolton
March 24, 1843	Part of Southborough annexed to Marlborough

Which version is easier to read and digest? The border lines of tables can be set to various widths and can even be made invisible to the reader.

Subheadings

Subheadings are essential to any online article divided into definable sections. This excerpt from Barbara Mathews' "Manuscript Family Records in Connecticut" (*NewEnglandAncestors.org*, February 1, 2002) shows just how effective they can be:

ANCESTRY SERVICE PEDIGREES AT THE
CONNECTICUT SOCIETY OF GENEALOGISTS

The Ancestry Service is a collection of the pedigree charts of members of the Connecticut Society of Genealogists. These are kept in three-ring binders at the Society's library in East Hartford and bound into a continuous set of volumes ordered by the membership number of the submitter. Three indexes cover the pedigrees, each focusing on a particular run of membership numbers. Each name in a pedigree chart is indexed to a membership number and the page within that member's pedigree chart. The index to the first series has been published. Currently, the Society's journal, *The Connecticut Nutmegger*, is publishing sections of the index to the first series in each issue.

The library of the Connecticut Society of Genealogists is open Monday through Friday, 9:30 a.m. to 4 p.m. It is open both to members and non-members alike.

Connecticut Society of Genealogists Library
175 Maple Street
East Hartford, Connecticut, 06033
860-569-0002

FAMILY FILES AT THE FERGUSON LIBRARY
The Ferguson Library in Stamford, Connecticut, is the "home" library of the Connecticut Ancestry Society. There are six file cabinet drawers of family files as well as a local history collection. The Connecticut Ancestry Society also houses a pedigree collection at the Ferguson, the contents of which were contributed by their members.

<u>The Ferguson Library</u>
One Library Place
Stamford, Connecticut, 06904
203-964-1000

THE JULIA BRUSH COLLECTION AT
THE CYRENIUS BOOTH LIBRARY
The public library in Newtown, Connecticut, is the repository of the Julia Emeline Clark Brush collection of genealogical materials. Items of interest include transcripts of probate, land, vital, cemetery, and town records for many surrounding towns in western Connecticut and eastern New York. There are also family files and local history scrapbooks. This collection is housed in the basement of the library.

<u>Cyrenius Booth Library</u>
25 Main Street
Newtown, Connecticut, 06470
203-426-2533

Note the clear division between each collection shown and the easy-to-locate contact information for each repository.

Images

Illustrations add a great deal to an article, whether online or on paper. Images should be pertinent to the article. It is never a good idea to add images that are not germane simply to have a picture included. Images should be free of copyright restrictions or the  author should obtain a written letter of consent from the copyright holder and send it to the website editor. Most web publishers will

GUIDELINES FOR FORMATTING YOUR ONLINE TEXT

Publishing online requires different formatting than traditional publishing techniques. Text does not display the same on a computer screen as it does on paper. The following guidelines will help you produce the best product.

Fonts

Serif fonts, such as Times New Roman, are the standard for print publishing. For electronic publishing, however, sans serif fonts should be used. Sans serif fonts are much more readable on a computer screen because the lines of the letters are cleaner without the serifs. Arial font is preferred and type should be 12 point for body copy (never more than 14 point, and never less than 10 point). Headlines can go as high as 14 point, but will likely read better at 12.

Underlining

Items on a web page that are underlined are hyperlinks to bring you to another page. Text should never be underlined unless it is meant to be a hyperlink. Doing so can cause extensive confusion for the reader.

Italics

Italicized fonts appear differently onscreen than they do in print. Limited italics can be used to bring emphasis; but extended italics should not be used in electronic publications. When the situation warrants, however, standard rules of grammar, such as italicizing the names of published works, should be followed.

All Caps/Small Caps

Using all caps online make the text stand out dramatically. IT IS THE EQUIVALENT OF SHOUTING! It is very harsh and difficult to read. Extended text should never be set as all caps or small caps.

HELP WITH WRITING FOR YOUR OWN WEBSITE

Creating a website gets easier with each passing year. Numerous software packages are available to assist you in creating your own website. Those who are new to the process, however, may need help with standard conventions for website publishing. The following two books are user-friendly and not overly technical, but will assist you in writing and formatting your own website.

Robin Williams and John Tollett
The Non-Designer's Web Book, 3rd ed.
(Berkeley, Cal.: Peachpit Press, 2006)

Williams and Tollett bring website design down to the basics that will assist you in creating great user-friendly pages that will communicate your writing most effectively.

Steve Krug
Don't Make Me Think: A Common Sense Approach to Web Usability, 2nd ed.
(Indianapolis, Ind.: New Riders, 2006)

This book is a must-have for anyone who is putting together their own website. Whether doing it on your own or with professional assistance, the principles outlined in this book will make it a great deal easier for users to be able to read your articles.

37Signals
Defensive Design for the Web: How to Improve Error Messages, Help, Forms, and Other Crisis Points
(Indianapolis, Ind.: New Riders, 2006)

While this book is slightly more technical, the section on Language Matters can be of great assistance to all writers. It also gives great tips for working with images on websites.

ask that images be sent in TIFF format via email or on disk. Images should be scanned at a resolution no lower than 300 dpi.

Endnotes

When submitting an article, all source citations should be listed at the end of the document as endnotes. Do not insert between paragraphs or at the end of individual pages. It makes the text more difficult to read. Website editors use both endnotes and footnotes, depending on the style guidelines for their site and the need of a particular article.

Checklist for "Writing for *NewEnglandAncestors.org* and Other Websites"

☑ Is the article the appropriate length?

☑ Does the article include subheadings for easy division?

☑ Are there hyperlinks to other resources?

☑ Is information presented as a table or bulleted list where appropriate?

☑ Are there images to accompany the article?

☑ Are all images copyright-free, or do you have a signed permission letter from the copyright holder?

☑ Are all images scanned at 300 dpi?

☑ Are sources documented and cited as endnotes, not footnotes?

CHAPTER FIVE

Writing Genealogical Books

Michael J. Leclerc

I f you're thinking about writing a genealogical book, you're join-ing a centuries-old American tradition. One of the first published genealogies in America, a broadside of the Rudolph Bollinger family, was published in 1743 at Ephrata Cloister, Lancaster County, Pennsylvania. In 1771 a genealogy of the Stebbins family was published in Hartford, Connecticut, the oldest known geneal-ogy in book form published in New England. The mid-1840s saw an increase in published genealogies in the United States; by World War I the number of published books had increased tenfold. The American Bicentennial in 1976 sparked an interest in American and family history, which sent the number of publications skyrocketing.

Since the mid-1990s there has been a huge boom in the number of "how-to" guides published to help genealogical researchers learn new techniques. Improvements in computers and computer pro-grams make it even easier for people to write about their families or about research methodology. Publishing the information from your boxes and files of papers will allow others to retrace your steps more easily in the future and ensure easy access to information about your ancestors.

FIRST STEPS

Before you decide to write a book, step back and ask yourself the following questions:

- What is my central theme? Has someone else written on the same topic?
- Who is the audience for the book?

- If so, do I have anything else new to say about this topic?
- Will I be correcting previously published information?

To differentiate your book from others, most of the content of your book should be previously unpublished information. If someone else has already written a major genealogy about your family, consider writing a supplement that treats new lines and corrects errors in the earlier work. Think of different angles to broaden the audience for the book. For instance, you might add female lines to a compiled genealogy—or, if you're writing a how-to book, demonstrate how to use new record sets or research techniques.

Decide on a central theme for your book, and then develop it. Will you discuss the descendants of a Civil War soldier? Create a guide for researching ancestors in upstate New York? Think about creating a work that will have the widest possible audience.

One of the major questions to answer regarding compiling a genealogy of descendants of an immigrant ancestor is whether to include female lines. Many of the major publications of the late-nineteenth and early-twentieth centuries do not trace female lines past the births and marriages of daughters, occasionally listing the names of their children. Many modern genealogies, however, trace female lines of descent as well. There is no right or wrong answer. You must decide for yourself which road you wish to take.

Make sure you conduct a search of existing published materials. There is nothing worse than spending a year writing a book, only to discover that someone else published a book on the same topic two months before you started writing. In addition to checking books, look at journals and magazines as well. You don't want to put together a book that hinges on the identification of a seventeenth-century immigrant ancestor, only to discover that someone else discovered the origins and published the information years ago.

At some point early in the process, you will also need to decide whether you will self-publish your book or contract with a publisher. Self-publishing will require you to handle all of the details yourself, from production and layout to printing the book.

Vanity presses will publish books for most individuals willing to pay them; however, the amount of work they will put into finalizing your manuscript is usually far smaller than with other publishers. Many publishers have stringent requirements for the submission of manuscripts. Among other things, they will want to have an idea of potential costs as well as potential sales for your work.

At NEHGS and the Newbury Street Press, we consider the following during the publications process: *Presentation, Organization, Style Guidelines, Design,* and *Printing*.

Presentation

Before you sit down to write, think about the direction you want to take. Look at examples of books similar to yours to get an idea of different structural styles. How is the information presented to the reader?

Guidebooks generally take a step-by-step approach, leading readers through different techniques, often building on information presented in previous chapters. Appendixes may include documents, charts, or sample forms.

Family histories can take a number of formats:

- Compilation of descendants of an ancestor, either to the current day or for a certain number of generations.
- Collection of certain lines of descent from immigrant ancestors with siblings in each generation, but not following all lines completely.
- A funnel-shaped "all-my-ancestors" work that traces your pedigree. These are often published in *ahnentafel* format, with you as person 1, your father as person 2, your mother as person 3, etc.
- An "hourglass" format that traces both the ancestors and descendants of a single individual. The individual is usually

placed in the center of the work, at the focal point of the hourglass.

- Local history of a town or county with compiled genealogies of residents.

Alternatively, you may decide to write a family history or memoir that does not focus on genealogy but may include a compiled genealogy as one component of the book, say, as an appendix. For example, your book might be

- A family history incorporating family artifacts and documents, such as letters, diaries, family lore, etc.
- A family history placing ancestors in the context of their life and times.
- A biography or personal memoir of an individual.

Organization

Once you choose your overall presentation, write a table of contents, which will serve as a framework to guide your writing. Include all of the following in your table of contents, where appropriate:

Front matter
- List of abbreviations
- List of illustrations
- Acknowledgments
- Preface or foreword
- Introduction

Main text
- Chapter titles, including subheadings where appropriate

End matter
- Appendixes
- Glossary of terms
- Endnotes (which might appear at ends of chapters instead)
- Bibliography
- Index

All of the material that appears before the first chapter is called the front matter. This is where people should find information about the book that will help them use it. Much of the front matter may be numbered with lower-case Roman numerals instead of Arabic ones.

The introduction gives a brief explanation or summary of the book. A preface is a brief commentary by the author. It sometimes contains the acknowledgments. A preface written by someone other than the author (or editor) is called a foreword. An introduction gives a brief explanation or summary, and is usually longer than a preface; for instance, you might include an introduction to give historical background.

The chapter titles will not be written in stone at this point. In fact, during the process of writing the book, you will likely change most if not all of them. You may also rearrange their order as you write. Use the chapter titles to start your writing. As the chapters start to take shape, use subheads to separate themes within a chapter. You may decide to use several layers of subheads for more complex sections of text.

All of the information that appears after the main body of the book is called the end matter. This includes appendixes, glossaries, bibliographies, endnotes, and the index.

Appendixes usually contain additional explanatory materials that supplement the information in the chapters. Long stretches of text that are too long for the main body (such as transcriptions of wills or land records) are often included in appendixes.

Not every book has a glossary, but particularly if you're writing a guidebook, you might want to consider including one if you're defining many terms. This book, for example, contains a glossary of abbreviations that genealogists typically use in their writing.

A bibliography is a list of references for further consultation by the user. They are particularly useful for long books with many references. Compiled genealogies will usually contain hundreds, if not thousands, of references that have short listings for published works. A bibliography provides a single place for the reader to get the full bibliographic citation for any book mentioned in a note. It can also contain lists of books to consult for additional information on a topic.

Although creating an index can be hard work, an index is essential to any good genealogical work. And the process of indexing can also turn up inconsistencies or other problems in the text prior to publication. See Chapter 7, in which Alvy Ray Smith discusses how to use Microsoft® WORD to automate the indexing process.

Style Guidelines

One of the most difficult things to do when writing a book is to keep a consistent style during the long time it takes to write it. You may have to choose which of several variant spellings to use, each of which may be correct (such as *appendixes* and *appendices*). Whichever spelling you choose, you should stick with it throughout the entire book. When you are writing a compiled genealogy, do you refer to a couple as John and Mary (Jones) Smith or as John Smith and Mary Jones? Do you use series commas (commas before the *and* in a list of items) or not?

To help remember what styles you decide to establish, it's a good idea to develop your own style sheet early in the writing process. When you decide on certain stylistic issues, such as the following, add them to your style sheet:

- Standardized spellings
- Naming conventions for married couples
- Naming conventions for married women
- Grammatical choices
- Special situations (e.g., how to list and number adoptees in a compiled genealogy)

Your style sheet might be only a single page, or it might be a long document. The earlier in the process you put it together, the more grateful you will be in the end when you are dealing with questions and problems. Chapters 2 and 6 give additional tips on style.

Design

A good design can make the difference between a successful work and one with limited appeal. Remember that you are putting together your book to share information with others. The more pleasing the book looks and the easier it is to read, the more likely it is that others will enjoy your book and easily understand the contents. Unless you are an experienced book designer, you should get help in this area. If you are working with a publisher, the staff will generally put together the design for the book. The amount of influence an author or editor has on the book design varies from publisher to publisher.

A number of things go into book design, from the overall dimensions of the book to typographic decisions such as font face and size to the layout of running heads, page numbers, and illustrations. The appearance of running heads—headers that usually give the short title of the book on one page and the title of the chapter on the facing page—is crucial, as these heads allow readers to see where they are in the book at any given time.

Visuals are an important part of the book design as well. As you are writing, keep ideas in mind for illustrations in each chapter. In addition to illustrations, charts and sidebars can be used quite effectively to make the text look pleasing. Illustrations and charts should include captions to make them more understandable. Callout boxes (stretches of text removed from the context of the article or chapter and appearing in a much larger type size than the regular text) can help break up the page visually.

Printing

If you are working with a publisher, the publisher will probably collaborate with you on the printing, or even handle all the printing arrangements. The color, weight, and texture of the paper have a great impact on the finished product. Will the book be a paperback or a hardcover? If it is a hardcover, will it have a dust jacket, or endpapers? What color will the cover be? These are just some of the issues that need to be decided, and publishers will get price quotes from printers based on those decisions.

Modern technology, such as "print on demand" (see sidebar, next page) makes it possible for individuals to produce their own books, and to "self-publish" rather than signing a contract with a book publisher. While this can save money, remember that suddenly you will be responsible for many of the printing decisions. If you are a new author or editor, you might find it very difficult to wade through the process and ensure you have a quality book in the end.

Another factor in your decision will be warehousing. If you use a publisher, they will often store the bound books for you. If you decide to self-publish, you will be responsible for storing your own books. In addition, the full burden of marketing your book will fall on you. Print-on-demand can mitigate these burdens by printing hard copies only when they are ordered, thus eliminating the need to warehouse. Some print-on-demand companies also offer online stores to assist you in marketing your book.

Unfortunately, printers who offer print-on-demand services will not usually provide you with design assistance, editing, proofreading, or many of the other steps in creating a book. If they do offer these services, they will usually charge additional fees, which you should take into account when deciding which route you will take.

PRINT-ON-DEMAND WEBSITES

A number of websites will provide print-on-demand services for you. The amount of assistance you receive in preparing your manuscript for publication will vary. Below are several sites that you can investigate for print-on-demand. You can also use Internet search engines to find other companies that offer these services.

www.cafepress.com

www.lulu.com

www.iuniverse.com

www2.xlibris.com

NEHGS BOOKS AND NEWBURY STREET PRESS

NEHGS publishes books under two imprints: NEHGS Books and Newbury Street Press. Unfortunately, the Society is unable to publish every book that is submitted. Decision factors in publishing books include the number of books planned for production in a given year; the subject matter; the quality of the work; and the budget, including potential sales as well as expenses.

NEHGS Books

NEHGS publishes four to five books per year, mostly guidebooks, under this imprint. In addition to the book in your hands now, popular titles include the bestselling *Genealogist's Handbook for New England Research, Shaking Your Family Tree: A Basic Guide to Tracing Your Family's Genealogy*, and *A Guide to Massachusetts Cemeteries*. We also occasionally publish scholarly compilations of significance, such as Professor Roger Thompson's *Cambridge Cameos: Stories of Life in Seventeenth-Century New England*, as well as produce some limited-run works purchased mainly by libraries, such as *Hartford County, Connecticut, County Court Minutes Volumes 3 and 4—1663–1687, 1697.*

Newbury Street Press

The Newbury Street Press imprint was started in 1996 as the special publications imprint of the Society. Its mission is to produce quality compiled family histories of enduring significance to genealogists, historians, and other researchers. The Press produces ten to twelve books per year; most are privately sponsored. Newbury Street Press staff consult regularly with highly accomplished scholars in the field of genealogy, and devote a great deal of attention to the overall design of the book as a material object suitable for being passed down to future generations of a family.

Checklist for "Writing Genealogical Books"

☑ Develop an idea for a book with creative, new, useful contents.

☑ Examine samples of similar books.

☑ Review options for the structure of your book.

☑ Organize the book in a way that makes sense and is easy to read and follow.

☑ Develop a style sheet.

☑ Ask advice from colleagues and friends on all aspects of your book.

☑ Develop a list of potential illustrations.

☑ Create lists of terms, abbreviations, and other items for the end matter.

☑ Create a complete index.

☑ Decide whether to contract with a publisher or to self-publish.

☑ Discuss design and printing considerations with your publisher.

CHAPTER SIX

Writing and Style

Gabrielle Stone and Carolyn Sheppard Oakley

W hen writing any kind of work—book, magazine article, journal article—it is important to adhere to a set of guidelines for style. *The Chicago Manual of Style*, published by the University of Chicago Press, 15th edition, is the authoritative work on writing style within the publishing industry. This work not only reviews rules relating to grammar, spelling, and writing style, but it also explains the publishing process from manuscript preparation to printing and binding. At NEHGS, we have standardized our publishing process and style based on the concepts discussed in *The Chicago Manual of Style* and other related publications, such as Elizabeth Shown Mills, ed., *Professional Genealogy: A Manual for Researchers, Writers, Editors, Lecturers, and Librarians* (Baltimore: Genealogical Publishing Co., 2001) and Elizabeth Shown Mills, *Evidence! Citation and Analysis for the Family Historian* (Baltimore: Genealogical Publishing Co., 1997).

NEHGS encourages authors to submit proposals for *The New England Historical and Genealogical Register*, *New England Ancestors* magazine, *NewEnglandAncestors.org*, NEHGS electronic publications, NEHGS book publications, or Newbury Street Press. A good proposal will include the topic to be covered, an outline of the article or book, reasons why this article or book should be published (e.g., new discoveries about a seventeenth-century immigrant), and a writing sample. For an article the writing sample might include a previously published article. For a book, a sample chapter from the proposed book would be the best sample. You should also include a summary of your published works. If the work is accepted, the staff editor of the appropriate department will review with you the specific guidelines covered in other chapters of this book.

SUBMITTING MANUSCRIPTS

In general, text submitted to NEHGS for print publications should follow certain formatting guidelines:

1. Prepare your manuscript with the most current version of Microsoft® WORD.

2. Double-space the text, although this is not necessary for the *Register*, and number all pages sequentially.

3. Use 12-point Times New Roman font for the text.

4. Make note references in the body of the manuscript superscript.

5. At this time, for the *Register* only, footnotes should be created automatically and put in 10-point type. For *New England Ancestors* magazine, put your notes in 9-point type and position them at the end of your manuscript; do *not* use WORD's automatic footnoting feature. (N.B.: Automatic footnoting conflicts with the magazine's design software.)

6. Type only one space after periods, question marks, exclamation points, colons, and semicolons. Most computer typefaces, including Times New Roman, are proportionally spaced, and one space is enough to separate sentences visually.

7. Avoid overusing all capitals or underlines for emphasis. Instead, use boldface or italic type and limit such emphasis to a few words.

8. Add white space between blocks of copy to accentuate breaks in text.

9. Submit your manuscript in both hardcopy and electronic format. The printout should be on 8.5 x 11 paper, on one side only. Either email your files or submit them on a PC-compatible CD-ROM. Please contact the specific editor with any other questions regarding the transmittal of the text.

Artwork

When sending images (photographs, maps, illustrations, charts, etc.), please include a list of every item sent, a caption or description for each image, an explanation of where the image should be placed within the text, and the *image* itself in hard copy or electronic form. If submitting images in electronic format, discuss the project-specific guidelines with your editor before creating the image files. Please note that the way the image looks in the final product is based mainly on the quality of the original given to NEHGS to reproduce.

Text and Art Permissions

If you quote text from another source in your manuscript, be aware that in certain cases you must obtain permission to use that text. In all cases, direct and indirect quotations of the work of another author must be properly cited. Likewise, most images are subject to copyright, and permission to use the image must be obtained from the rights holder, unless you own the original image. This process can take months, so it is best to obtain permission as soon as possible. In addition, it is important to note that there are usually fees involved with obtaining permission for both text and art.

NEHGS editors can in some cases assist with the permissions process. For more information on copyright law, contact the United States Copyright Office, the Library of Congress, 101 Independence Avenue, S.E., Washington, D.C. 20559-6000; you can see guidelines online at *www.loc.gov/copyright*.

GENERAL STYLE GUIDELINES

It is beyond the scope of this book to enumerate every style issue you'll encounter in preparing a manuscript for submission. This section outlines some of the questions most frequently asked by genealogical authors. Please refer to the three references cited in the first paragraph for expanded explanations of these points, as well as answers to more general questions.

When should I use abbreviations?

It is preferable to use abbreviations sparingly, and when you are certain that all readers of the manuscript will be familiar with the abbreviation and its meaning. See Appendix A, Abbreviations and Acronyms.

Genealogical abbreviations or acronyms are formatted without spaces or periods:

NEHGS, FASG, CG

Do not abbreviate state names in running text. Postal abbreviations should be used only in mailing addresses.

Abbreviate *United States* only when using it as an adjective. Spell it out whenever it is used as a noun. The two-letter abbreviation for the United States of America (*U.S.*) uses periods.

How should I style dates?

For the *Register* and compiled genealogies, dates should be written in day-month-year order (*12 August 2006*). For all other NEHGS publications, dates should be written in month-day-year order (*August 12, 2006*). No comma is needed between a month and a year (*August 2006*). Commas are required after a year when month, day, and year (or day, month, and year) are used in text:

> She completed the project on May 25, 2006, and presented her findings to the staff on June 1, 2006.

Do not abbreviate months in running text. Numerical ordinals such as 1st or 2nd should not be used for days; however, they may be used for months in Quaker-style dates (*21 7th month 1784*).

Do not use an apostrophe when referring to decades (*the 1820s*). Centuries should be referred to in similar style (*the 1900s*).

When referring to a century, write out the words (*nineteenth century*); when describing something as belonging to a particular century, use a hyphen (*nineteenth-century family Bible* or *mid-nineteenth-century family history*).

What is the best way to write gender-neutral text?

The best way to write copy that applies equally to males and females is to use plurals. For example:

To be successful, researchers need to attend lectures and practice good organizational skills.

If it is not possible to use plurals, join the pronouns with a conjunction:

If a student is unable to attend the program, he or she should notify the education department immediately.

In some instances, it may be preferable to recast the sentence in the passive voice, even though you should normally avoid using it.

What are the conventions for styling names?

Use a space between two initials. Style three initials or more without spaces between letters.

J. T. Smith, C.S.D. Jones, and L. Johnson spoke at the meeting.

Jr. or Sr. should be preceded and followed by a comma, but commas are not used with Roman or Arabic numerals—unless personal preference differs.

Robert S. Brown, Jr.
Carl B. Taylor III

Carefully double-check the spelling and styling of all names, including personal preferences. Your editor and proofreader may not be familiar with the names in your manuscript and will have difficulty identifying spelling errors.

When should I spell out numbers and when should I use numerals?

In general, spell out whole numbers from one through one hundred. Remember to hyphenate where necessary (*twenty-one* through *twenty-nine*, etc.). Spell out whole numbers from one through one hundred when they are followed by hundred, thousand, hundred thousand, etc.

Do not observe this rule so strictly that the text becomes inconsistent within a sentence or passage. In reporting ages from a census record, for example, use figures or words consistently throughout.

What frequently used words with alternate spellings should I watch for?

The growth of technology during the past years has brought several new words into the English language, many of which have several different spellings. NEHGS has tried to standardize certain spellings as follows:

> email
> Internet
> online
> website, the Web, World Wide Web

How should I style website and email addresses?

Use standard punctuation when a website address ends a sentence. Most Internet users will be familiar with the basic structure of an address.

Italicize website and email addresses, and, except for parentheses, do not hyperlink or use enclosures for them. Remove any automatic hyperlinking before submitting your manuscript.

Do not add punctuation to an email or Internet address. Do not hyphenate it unless it contains a long word that might naturally break with a hyphen.

Omit "http://" at the beginning of addresses and forward slashes at the end. Most browsers will automatically insert these. This also applies to web addresses that do not begin with "www."

What are the rules for capitalization?

Capitalization should not be excessive. Generic nouns such as "census" or "tax" or "federal" need not be capitalized, even when used to designate a particular case (e.g., the 1930 U.S. census).

Capitalize a title only when it forms a word group with a following proper noun, even in the same sentence.

> Abraham Lincoln was president of the United States.

> The crowd stood when President Lincoln entered the room.

Sailors serving under Admiral Nimitz in World War II often heard the admiral talk frankly.

What are the rules for titles of works?

Words in the titles of works in English should all have initial capitals except for articles (unless the first word of the title or subtitle), coordinating conjunctions, and prepositions. It is permissible to correct capitalization of titles. It is also permissible to correct or add punctuation to titles. When you add something to a title, place it in square brackets.

Italicize titles of published works (books, periodicals). Titles of articles, chapters of books, and unpublished works are enclosed in quotation marks and are not italicized:

Robert Charles Anderson, George F. Sanborn Jr., and Melinde Lutz Sanborn, *The Great Migration: Immigrants to New England, 1634–1635, Volume I, A–B* (Boston: NEHGS, 1999).

David Jay Webber, "Major William[2] Bradford's Second Wife: Was She the Widow of Francis[2] Griswold?" *Register* 155 (2001):245–50.

John Pynchon, "Hampshire Records of Births: Marriages [&] Deaths," manuscript at the Connecticut Valley Historical Museum, Springfield, Massachusetts.

How should I format quotations?

Indent long quotations within the text on one or both sides; do not use quotation marks.

Indicate omissions by using context-sensitive ellipsis points, separated by spaces. For example, an omission from within a sentence is indicated by three points, which always remain together on a single line of text. Omissions that run over one or more sentence boundaries, on the other hand, will require four points, the first of which follows the last word without a space and indicates a period. In general, ellipsis points are not required at the beginning or end of quotations.

When do I use hyphens, en dashes, and em dashes?

A hyphen (-) joins two words into one.

An en dash (–) expresses a range of numbers or years.

An em dash (—) signifies a major break in thought.

When writing inclusive numbers (such as pages or years), carry over all the digits that change and include at least two digits for the second number (unless in a different century). Such inclusive numbers use an en dash.

pages 26–29, 147–53, 1004–05
years 1887–1915 and 1919–27

An em dash should be set off with a space on either side.

What about other punctuation?

Volumes have been written about punctuation. Again, a guide such as *The Chicago Manual of Style* will prove useful. What follows is a summary of some of the particular issues encountered in genealogical writing.

Colons

A list or a quotation should be introduced by a colon. Capitalize material after a colon if it forms a complete sentence.

Commas

Commas should always be used sparingly within the text. NEHGS uses the series comma (e.g., *French, English, and Italian*—rather than *French, English and Italian*).

Terms or phrases that are essential for conveying the meaning of the sentence should not be enclosed by commas.

The family arrived in 1906 on the ship *Mauretania*.

But commas are needed when a term or phrase is not essential for conveying the meaning of the sentence.

Robert Brown, who was the testator's nephew, was named executor in the will.

The use of *that* and *which* follows comparable rules:

> The boat that arrived yesterday was on time.

> The *Mauretania*, which was built in 1900, made its maiden voyage in 1901.

A clause that begins a sentence should end with a comma.

> Once Hans made up his mind to emigrate, he could not turn back.

A single place name does not need commas. But a two-part place name needs two commas.

> Thomas Ray settled in Ipswich in 1645.

> Robert Stokes emigrated from Leek, Staffordshire, in 1828.

A comma can be used to show where the break is in a string of words that otherwise could have more than one meaning.

> Soon after, the meeting settled down to business.

Quotation marks and apostrophes

Be careful to use true "curly" single (' ') and double (" ") quotation marks and apostrophes, rather than the symbols for foot and inch.

Commas and periods should usually be placed inside double quotation marks. Colons, semicolons, and question marks should be placed outside double quotation marks.

Semicolons

Use semicolons to separate items in a list that includes commas and to separate closely related clauses in a sentence.

Brackets

Use square brackets to indicate you are adding words or comments to a source or quotation.

Checklist for "Writing and Style"

Before submitting text to NEHGS be sure to:

☑ Review and adhere to style, grammar, and spelling guidelines outlined in this text and in the references cited in the first paragraph.

☑ Review the nine points under "Submitting Manuscripts."

☑ List any artwork by title, description, source, and placement within text.

☑ Obtain any text and art permissions.

☑ Review the General Style Guidelines.

☑ Review any separate guidelines covered in other chapters of this book.

CHAPTER SEVEN

Writing Using WORD for Genealogy: Utilizing Microsoft® WORD in Genealogical Documents in *Register,* or Modified *Register* [NGSQ], Format

by Alvy Ray Smith[1]

Genealogists are generally unaware of the power built into Microsoft® WORD that is directly applicable to their field. This chapter will demonstrate a set of WORD techniques that greatly ease the burden of writing papers or books in *Register,* or Modified *Register* [NGSQ], format. The techniques can be easily added to already existing documents.

Renumbering a document is a form of torture unnecessarily endured by authors of genealogies. An insertion or deletion of a family member necessitates a renumbering, regardless of the format used. This is particularly noisome when *Register* format is used, Modified [NGSQ][2] or not, because the numbering is cumulative; a change in

---

[1] This article originally appeared as a series in *New England Ancestors* magazine in the following issues: Summer 2004, vol. 5, no. 3, pp. 50–53; Fall 2004, vol. 5, no. 4, pp. 51–54; Holiday 2004, vol. 5, nos. 5–6, pp. 59–60; Winter 2005, vol. 6, no. 1, pp. 50–51, 54. The author is greatly indebted to Marsha Hoffman Rising, CG, FASG, and Robert Charles Anderson, FASG, for help in debugging this complex document.

[2] There is controversy about the naming of this format, which is also called Jacobus, *Record* format (for *The New York Genealogical and Biographical Record*), or NGSQ format (for the *National Genealogical Society Quarterly*). Since the NGSQ terminology is highly favored today by a substantial number of important genealogists, I have elected to show

the early parts of the document ramify throughout the entire document. Here I will show how simple techniques built into WORD obviate the need for renumbering forever.[3] And these techniques apply to all numbered items in a document, not just persons—for example, illustrations and appendixes.

Genealogy documents can become cumbersome, especially the larger ones. The well-known hyperlinks commonly used on the Internet also can be used *inside* a WORD document. These links can be made invisible to readers of the document, and they greatly ease the author's task of creating the document in the first place. For example, it becomes trivial with hyperlinks to jump from the sketch of a child to the sketch of its parent and back. You, as an author, no longer have to remember where these bits of text reside in the document, nor is a search for keywords required; a simple click just takes you there.

Another class of problems, particularly in larger documents, are called table-generation problems—for example, of tables of contents, illustrations, names, and places—where page numbers are attached to specific items. WORD techniques are available to generate these automatically, the correct page numbers being inserted automatically by WORD.

AUTOMATIC NUMBERING AND RENUMBERING

There are two fundamental WORD skills required for enabling your document to automatically renumber. You must understand bookmarking, and you must know how to insert a sequenced number. After the general techniques are introduced, they will be applied to a document in *Register* format, and also to one in Modified *Register* [NGSQ] format.

---

that name also every time I use the Modifed *Register* name, so that there is no confusion about my intent.

[3] Henceforth WORD will signify Microsoft® WORD in all its many versions, a product of the Microsoft Corporation. The version I use for all examples is Microsoft® WORD 2002, running under the Microsoft® Windows XP operating system. Some modification of procedures described herein may be required for other versions. Illustrations are done in Microsoft® WORD 2003, runing under the Microsoft® Windows XP operating system.

Bookmarks. A bookmark is a named location in your document. You can place a bookmark anywhere you want. For example, in a sketch for Preserved Partridge, my fictitious genealogical patriarch, I might want to bookmark his name so that I can easily jump to his sketch from elsewhere in the document. I would click next to his name to indicate where I want to place a bookmark. I might click directly left of his name, for example, or I might select his entire name, meaning that I want the bookmark to be associated with this occurrence of his name.

To insert a bookmark, click on Insert: Bookmark[4] *(Fig. 1)* and add a name of your invention for the bookmark in the box provided.

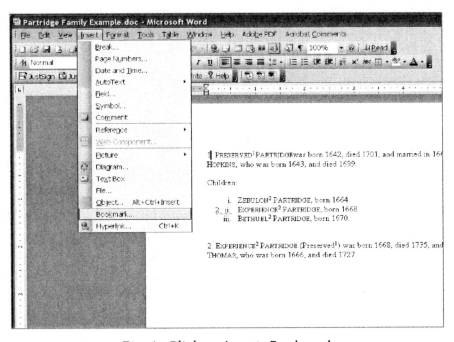

Fig. 1. Click on Insert: Bookmark

---

[4] This abbreviates the wordy sequence: Click on Insert (in the menu bar near the top of the window); then click on Bookmark. Using this technique, the entire sequence in this paragraph could be abbreviated to: Click on Insert: Bookmark: *PreservedPartridge*: Add. Regular sans serif typeface indicates Word commands or dialog box labels, and *italic sans serif* typeface denotes invented strings of text or numbers that you provide.

Then click **Add**. I might choose for a bookmark name, in this example, *PreservedPartridge*. The only real requirement is that the name be unique among your bookmarks. IMPORTANT—*A bookmark cannot have embedded spaces.* So *Preserved Partridge* is not allowed, but *Preserved_Partridge* is *(Fig. 2)*.

Fig. 2. Add a name of your invention for the bookmark in the box provided, then click **Add**.

Sequenced numbers. To insert a sequenced number means to insert the next number, whatever it is, into a desired location, without you yourself having to know what that number actually is. Different sequences have different names, so that WORD can distinguish between them. For example, a sequence of persons might be called *Person*, a sequence of children *Child*, a sequence of illustrations *Figure*, and a sequence of appendixes *Appendix*. Generally, this is accomplished by clicking on **Insert: Field: Seq**, then editing the command to contain the desired sequence name. Let's step through this:

In your document click on a position where you want to insert an automatic number. Then click on **Insert: Field** *(Fig. 3)*. You must then choose the **Field** name called **Seq** in the list displayed. An easier way to do this is to first choose from **Categories** (use the down arrow to see the list) the sequence type called **Numbering**, then **Seq** is easier to find in the shortened list under **Field names**. You may skip this last step, but you will have to scroll down through a long list of names to find **Seq** *(Fig. 4)*.

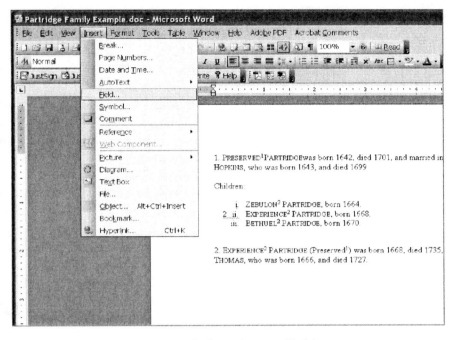

Fig. 3. Click on Insert: Field.

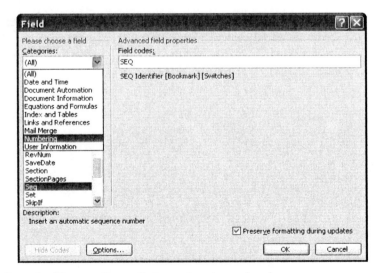

Fig. 4. Choose from Categories *(use the down arrow to see the list) the sequence type called* Numbering, *then* Seq *is easier to find in the shortened list under* Field *names.*

Now you will want to edit the field command that you are preparing to enter into your document. You will not see the command (in the document) but only its effects. To edit, click on the button **Field Codes**, which opens up an editing box with the word SEQ already typed in and labeled **Field codes.**[5] You will type the name of your sequence next to that word. (WORD automatically inserts a space for you after SEQ.) For example, here is where you might type the word *Person* for your automatic person sequence. Of course, you can see the command in this editing box *(Fig. 5)*.

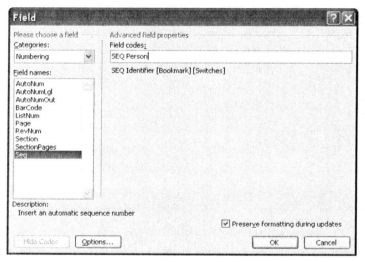

Fig. 5. Type the name of your sequence
next to the word SEQ *in the* Field Code.

In general you will now want to add some formatting instructions to your field command, but in the simplest case, this is not necessary. Be sure that the box next to **Preserve formatting during updates** is checked.[6] When you are done, simply click **OK**. The next number in

---

[5] In some versions of Word, you will not have to click on a button to get this editing box to appear. It will just be there, labeled **Field codes.**

[6] This inserts an option called *MERGEFORMAT, so don't be surprised if you stumble onto that one. It simply means to use the formatting in the vicinity of the inserted number. For example, if the text in the vicinity of the

the (named) sequence will automatically appear where you inserted this command. It would be an Arabic number in this case because that is the default without explicit formatting instructions. It will start at 1 if you have not told it otherwise with a special formatting instruction. In the examples below, formatting will be further explained.

Example 1. Suppose our first sketch in *Register* format is devoted to Preserved Partridge. Our goal is never to use an explicit person number, only automatically generated person numbers (or fields that will be shaded in gray[7]). We might wish a brief sketch to look like this:

> 1. PRESERVED[1] PARTRIDGE was born 1642, died 1701, and married in 1664 CHARITY HOPKINS, who was born 1643, and died 1699.

When I entered this sketch, I did not type the leading 1. I started the paragraph with the period that would follow the number and then typed the rest of the paragraph. Then I clicked just left of the leading period where I wanted an automatic number to be inserted. Here I invoked the skill for insertion of automatic numbers described above and entered the command

SEQ *Person*

via the sequence described above: Click on Insert: Field: Seq: Field Codes. Then I typed the word *Person* next to the word *SEQ*, and clicked OK. The Arabic numeral 1 appears automatically *(Fig. 6)*.

I could have *forced* the 1 by the command

---

inserted number is boldface, then the inserted number will be boldface. This is usually what you want to happen.

[7] To make this parenthetical phrase true, click on Tools: Options and set Field shading to Always. Then click OK. Alternatively, you can set Field shading to When selected, in which case, a field will be shaded in gray only when you select it. I recommend Always, but if you also have Bookmarks checked, then you might opt to go with When selected. Otherwise the field shading can mask the Bookmarks indicators (gray [and] brackets).

SEQ *Person*\r*1*

which resets the named sequence to the number following the \r.[8]

Example 2. Now let's add children to Preserved's sketch. We will use the sequenced number skill several times, in several variations, to accomplish this. Suppose we want the full sketch to look like this, in *Register* format (Modified *Register* [NGSQ] will be explained in the following example):

> 1. PRESERVED[1] PARTRIDGE was born 1642, died 1701, and married in 1664 CHARITY HOPKINS, who was born 1643, and died 1699.
>
>   Children:
>   i. Zebulon[2] Partridge, born 1664.
>   2. ii. Experience Partridge, born 1668.
>   iii. Bethuel Partridge, born 1670.

Since daughter Experience is to be expanded into her own sketch, she is given the next successive person number. You should be able to do this by now. Simply insert, where you want her number to appear, the command

SEQ *Person*

(assuming that I no longer need to explain all the clicking and typing that this really means).

Now we apply the sequenced number skill in new ways. In the numbered list of children there are two things to notice: (1) The list always restarts from i in every sketch; and (2) the numbers are lowercase Roman numerals.

The command to use for the first child in such a list is

SEQ *Child* \r*1**roman

---

[8] Word does not distinguish case in these commands, and spaces are not required before or after switches, so these commands could be equivalently written seq *person*, and seq *person*\r*1*, respectively.

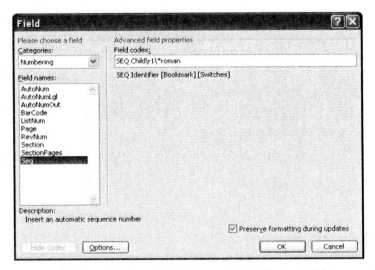

Fig. 6. Click on Insert: Field: Seq: Field Codes. *Then type the word* Person *next to the word* SEQ, *and click* OK.

where I have arbitrarily chosen the name *Child* for this special type of sequenced number.[9] I don't want this sequence of numbers to interfere with my main person numbering scheme—the *Person* numbers. You can choose any name you want, of course.

Since the numbering must restart at i in each sketch, I have explicitly supplied the \r*1* formatting instruction to the command *(Fig. 7)*. If you have trouble remembering this, you can find the formatting commands in the dialog box for Insert: Field: Seq: Field Codes: Options: Field Specific Switches. Click on \r and—VERY IMPORTANT—click on Add to Field to insert the switch into the command being constructed in the editing box. This step is very easy to overlook, and I cannot overemphasize the care you should take not to skip it. You will get unexpected results if you do, and such unexpected results should immediately alert you to the possibility that you forgot to Add to Field. You will also have to explicitly type the *1* (or other desired start number) after the switch \r. Then click OK. No space has to separate the \r from the *1*, but I use one anyway.

---

[9] As previously indicated, this command could be written equivalently seq *child*\r*1**roman.

To format the number as a lower-case Roman numeral, either explicitly type the formatting command * roman as shown or perform this sequence: Click on Insert: Field: Seq: Field Codes: Options: General Switches: Formatting: i, ii, iii, . . . *(Fig. 8).* Don't forget to click Add to Field before you click OK! No space has to separate * from roman, but I use one anyway.

Now back to Preserved's sketch: The other two children are easy. Just insert in the appropriate places the command

SEQ *Child* * roman

where the only difficulty might be forgetting to format for lower-case Roman numerals, or forgetting to click the Add to Field button.

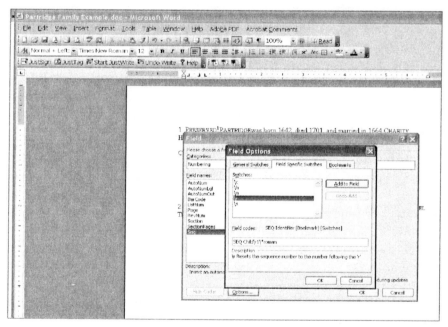

Fig. 7. You can find the formatting commands in the dialog box for Insert: Field: Seq: Field Codes: Options: Field Specific Switches. *Click on* \r *and—VERY IMPORTANT—click on* Add to Field *to insert the switch into the command being constructed in the editing box.*

Example 3. Same as the example above but for Modified *Register* [NGSQ] format in which every person gets a number, whether expanded into a separate sketch or not, a plus sign (+) indicating expansion into a separate sketch:

   1. PRESERVED[1] PARTRIDGE was born 1642, died 1701, and married in 1664 CHARITY HOPKINS, who was born 1643, and died 1699.

    Children:

    2.   i. ZEBULON[2] PARTRIDGE, born 1664.

+ 3. ii. EXPERIENCE PARTRIDGE, born 1668.

    4. iii. BETHUEL PARTRIDGE, born 1670.

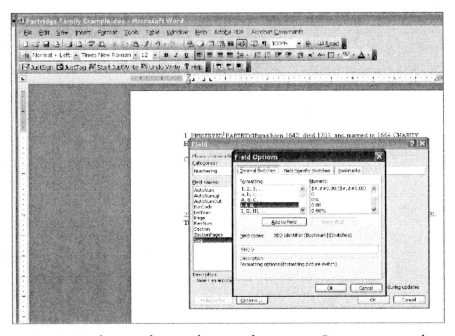

Fig. 8. To format the number as a lower-case Roman numeral, either explicitly type the formatting command * roman as shown or perform this sequence: Click on Insert: Field: Seq: Field Codes: Options: General Switches: Formatting: i, ii, iii, ...

The only difference between this and the previous example is that two additional *Person* numbers need to be inserted, for Zebulon and Bethuel, using the by now well-known command

SEQ *Person*

The *Child* numbering is exactly the same as before.

Example 4. Adding a sketch for Experience Partridge requires use of the bookmarking skill and brings the full power of automatic renumbering into play. Suppose Experience's sketch will look like this, in *Register* format:

2. EXPERIENCE[2] PARTRIDGE (*Preserved[1]*) was born 1668, died 1735, and married SAMUEL THOMAS, who was born 1666, and died 1727.

It is important that the number of this sketch match the number in the list of children in Preserved's sketch, even if that number changes (and we will change it in an example below). The rule that will be followed is this: After the first sketch, we introduce new numbers only in children lists, never in person, or sketch, lists. So how do we get the number 2 above to automatically insert itself in Experience's sketch?

The main technique involves the use of a bookmark, followed by use of a field command referencing that bookmark. The first step is to bookmark every child who is to be expanded into a separate sketch. In this case, we have one such child, child ii in the sketch for Preserved Partridge. In that line select the *Person* number field (the 2, not the ii) and insert a bookmark for it by clicking on Insert: Bookmark and inserting a name for the bookmark. IMPORTANT — Be sure to put a space between the word *Person* and your bookmark name *(Fig. 9)*. For this example I invented the bookmark name *EXPERIENCEofPRESERVED*. I tend to be wordy so that I will have no difficulty picking out a particular bookmark later when I might have hundreds of them in my document. If you know there will be only one Experience in your document, you might simply call the bookmark *Experience* or *EXPERIENCE*. What you have done is to associate this bookmark with the automatically generated number assigned to Experience in the list of children under Preserved.

IMPORTANT — The instruction above is to select the *Person* number field before inserting a bookmark for it. This means exactly what it says: Select the entire number field. WORD will do the right thing if you click just left of the number field, but it will fail (in a way that is very difficult to debug) if you simply click some arbitrary place on the line to insert the bookmark. I recommend you select the entire field. One way to do this is to push down the left mouse button with the cursor just to the left of the number and then drag the cursor to the right until the entire field is highlighted, then release the mouse button and insert the bookmark to be associated with this selection.

Now we will use the new bookmark to number Experience's own sketch. Click on the position where this number is to appear to the left of the first line of Experience's sketch. Then insert the command

SEQ *Person EXPERIENCEofPRESERVED*

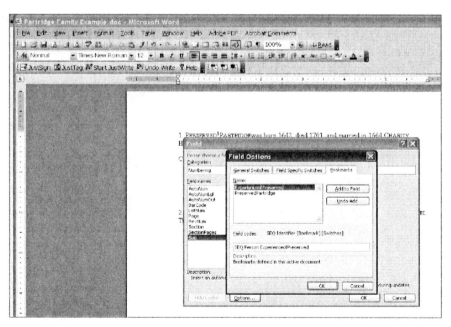

Fig. 9. Select the Person number *field (the 2, not the ii) and insert a bookmark for it by clicking on* Insert: Bookmark *and inserting a name for the bookmark. IMPORTANT—Be sure to put a space between the word* Person *and your bookmark name.*

in the usual way, but with one addition. That is, click on **Insert: Field: Seq: Field Codes**, and then type the word *Person* after the word **SEQ**, which is already provided. Then either type the bookmark name from memory, or click on the **Options** button, then click on **Bookmarks**, then find the desired bookmark in the list supplied, and click on it. Then — VERY IMPORTANT — click **Add to Field** before clicking **OK**. This will cause the number associated with the specified bookmark to be inserted in the desired position. That's the magic of automatic renumbering. If, for some reason, the number assigned to child Experience changes, then the number of her sketch will automatically renumber too.

Example 5. Same as the example above but for Modified *Register* [NGSQ] format:

> 3. EXPERIENCE[2] PARTRIDGE (*Preserved*[1]) was born 1668, died 1735, and married SAMUEL THOMAS, who was born 1666, and died 1727.

Exactly the same technique is used here as in the example immediately above. Since the automatic number generated in the Modified [NGSQ] case is a 3 instead of a 2, the number 3 automatically appears as the number for Experience's sketch.

You now know the basics of automatic numbering. Let's exercise the scheme with an example requiring a renumbering. You will see that no renumbering work is involved at all!

Example 6. Here we insert a new second child, resulting from some recently acquired research on the family of Preserved Partridge:

> 1. PRESERVED[1] PARTRIDGE was born 1642, died 1701, and married in 1664 CHARITY HOPKINS, who was born 1643, and died 1699.
>
> Children:
> > i. ZEBULON[2] PARTRIDGE, born 1664.
> 2. ii. PATIENCE PARTRIDGE, born 1666.
> 3. iii. EXPERIENCE PARTRIDGE, born 1668.
> > iv. BETHUEL PARTRIDGE, born 1670.

I actually did no insertion of commands to effect this change. I simply copied the line containing Experience and then pasted it, in the same place. Then I changed the name Experience to Patience in the new second line, and changed the date to 1666. This works because the correct fields for the numbers have already been inserted and they were faithfully copied when I did the copy and paste. IMPORTANT: *To see the automatic renumbering, you must cause the fields to be updated.* To do this, select the lines that will be affected, and then click F9. The safest thing to do is to select the entire document (Edit: Select All will do this, or click in the main text and type Control + A), then click F9. This regenerates all the number fields in the document.

Do not copy the first line, Zebulon's line, because it contains the embedded command

SEQ *Child*\r1*roman

which resets the Child number to i. You *can* copy and paste any of the other children's lines, but choose one that has the same fields as you wish to appear in the new line.

Of course, you can always resort to entering by hand the SEQ commands as described earlier, but once crucial parts of a document are established, such as the first sketch, then much can be accomplished with just copy and paste.

When the sketch for Experience Partridge is updated (by selecting it and clicking F9), its number automatically becomes a 3. No work on the author's part is required. The author's work is to add a sketch for Patience Partridge, using the numbering techniques already described.

Example 7. Same as the example above but for Modified *Register* [NGSQ] format:

1. PRESERVED[1] PARTRIDGE was born 1642, died 1701, and married in 1664 CHARITY HOPKINS, who was born 1643, and died 1699.

Children:

2.   i. ZEBULON[2] PARTRIDGE, born 1664.

+ 3. ii. PATIENCE PARTRIDGE, born 1666.

+ 4. iii. EXPERIENCE PARTRIDGE, born 1668.

5. iv. BETHUEL PARTRIDGE, born 1670.

Exactly the same technique works for Modified *Register* [NGSQ] format. The only difference in this case is that, after updating the document (with **Select All** and **F9**), the sketch for Experience will automatically be renumbered 4.

UPDATING EXISTING DOCUMENTS

Suppose you have a genealogical document you've written in the past that is, say, fifty pages long or so, long enough that you would not want to retype it. You will be happy to learn that the techniques from Part 1 can be added to your old document without having to rewrite it. Here is a suggested set of steps for "modernizing" your document to take advantage of the techniques described last time:

1. First do the Arabic numbers (that is, insert **SEQ** *Person*) for the first sketch (only) and for the children in all the sketches. This directive means for all the children in the paper if using Modified *Register* [NGSQ] format, but only all those that have further sketches if using the *Register* system. Just select an automatic Arabic number you have created. Copy it with **Control + C**, then paste it with **Control + V** where Arabic numbers used to be.[10] Be sure to delete the numbers you had typed there previously. Note that all Arabic numbers will be the same until you update the entire manuscript with **Control + A** (or **Edit: Select All**) then **F9**. Click **Update entire table**, if asked, then **OK** in that case. (Let's call this procedure an Update All.) Note that the numbers for sketches are not changed in this step (except for the first one).

2. Next enter bookmarks for each child who is to be expanded into a sketch. This directive means for each child line with a + sign if

---

[10] **Edit: Copy** and **Edit: Paste** accomplish the same thing.

using Modified *Register* [NGSQ] format, or only those child lines with an Arabic number if using the *Register* format. Do so by selecting the Arabic number field on each child line of a child to be expanded. Then insert a unique bookmark there.

3. In this step the sketch numbers are made automatic. Link each child sketch to the corresponding child line in its parents' sketch. Do so by selecting the Arabic number at the beginning of each sketch [after the first, which was numbered in step 1] and inserting there **SEQ** *Person* [*bookmarkname*], where [*bookmarkname*] represents the unique bookmark you created for the corresponding child in step 2. You can tell that this step has been done by the presence of a gray field surrounding the sketch's number.[11] [Hint: You might want to insert hyperlinks while you do this step — see the next section. This is a great time to do it, and it lets you check immediately to see whether you've correctly linked child to parent and vice versa.]

4. Now create all the "first" child numbers in all sketches — that is, the children with lowercase Roman numeral i. Create the first child's number explicitly by inserting [**SEQ** *Child*\r1* roman] in the proper place in the first child line of the first sketch with children. Then select and copy that field (with **Control + C**) and paste it (with **Control + V**) into the proper position in the first child line of all other sketches with children.

5. Then go back and create the "non-first" child numbers in all sketches — that is, the children with lowercase Roman numerals greater than i. Find the first sketch in the paper with more than one child. Create the first "non-first" child's number explicitly by inserting [**SEQ** *Child**roman] in the proper place in the child line of the second child of that sketch. Then select and copy that field (with **Control + C**) and paste it (with **Control + V**) into the proper position in the child lines of all non-first children in other sketches with children. Note that the roman numerals will all be the same until you do an Update All.

---

[11] Recall that this step requires that you have turned on field shading with **Tools: Options: View: Field shading: Always**.

Marsha Hoffman Rising, an early user[12] of the techniques here, reported that it took her about an hour to automatically number a 165-page manuscript.

TROUBLESHOOTING

- If nothing happens when you think you have completed the steps, you probably have forgotten the VERY IMPORTANT Add to Field.

- If you get an error message: *Error! No sequence specified.*, you have forgotten *Person* or *Child* or whatever you have named your number sequence.

- If you get a field (a gray square) but it has no number, you have forgotten to put a number after the \r switch in \r*roman. Forgetting to specify a number for \r usually generates a 0, but in Roman numerals a zero is undefined so you get a blank.

- If your sketch numbers don't match the corresponding child numbers after an Update All, then you have made a mistake entering the bookmark in the child's line. Perhaps you did not enter it just left of, or atop, the *Person* number field there. Or you forgot an Add to Field.

- There is a WORD trick (already mentioned in a footnote) to know if you are having trouble with bookmarks. Turn on the checkbox next to Tools: Options: View: Bookmarks (under Show), which will display gray [and] brackets around each bookmark you have inserted. Field shading can interfere with the visibility of these marks, which are also gray. In general, then, it is a good idea to turn off Field shading with Tools: Options: View: Never, while looking for bookmarks. The brackets will overlap, forming a large uppercase I, if the bookmark is located at a selected point rather than over a selected area *(Figs. 10–11)*.

---

[12] In the software industry we call these people "beta-testers." They have to endure very buggy code, but they get first crack at it. It is sometimes worth the pain.

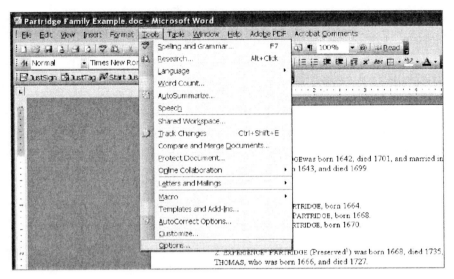

Fig. 10. Select Tools: Options.

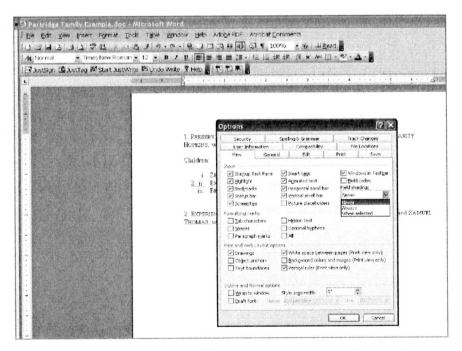

Fig. 11. Turn on the checkbox next to Tools: Options: View:
Bookmarks (under Show), *which will display gray [and] brackets
around each bookmark you have inserted.*

INTERNAL HYPERLINKS

The bookmarking skill from the previous lesson can be extended to internal hyperlinks. These allow an author to skip around in convenient ways through a large document without having to remember or search. For example, suppose that the sketch for Preserved Partridge above was fifty or a hundred pages long, instead of two lines long. Then the sketch for Experience would be located in the document a long way from the sketch for Preserved. In genealogy documents it is often convenient to skip back and forth between a parents' sketch and sketches for their children, and then from each of these sketches to those for their children in turn. Hyperlinks make such movement easy.

Example 8. Here we will use bookmarks in both a parent and a child sketch to implement hyperlinks between them. Let's use the familiar sketches from before. I won't bother to use a separate example for Modified *Register* [NGSQ] format because exactly the same technique is used in either format.

> 1. PRESERVED[1] PARTRIDGE was born 1642, died 1701, and married in 1664 CHARITY HOPKINS, who was born 1643, and died 1699.
>
>   Children:
>
> > i. ZEBULON[2] PARTRIDGE, born 1664.
>
> 2. ii. EXPERIENCE PARTRIDGE, born 1668.
>
> > iii. BETHUEL PARTRIDGE, born 1670.

. . . [Assume many pages here to make this example meaningful.]

> 2. EXPERIENCE[2] PARTRIDGE (*Preserved[1]*) was born 1668, died 1735, and married SAMUEL THOMAS, who was born 1666, and died 1727.

We are already prepared to insert the first hyperlink because we have inserted a bookmark for child ii, Experience, in Preserved's sketch in the exercises before. Remember? We selected the *Person* number field in that line and inserted a bookmark there. That is, we associated a bookmark name with that number, which just so happens to be the child line for Experience corresponding to a sketch for Experience.

Now go to the sketch for Experience, select her name, EXPERIENCE[2] PARTRIDGE (select the whole name), and right-click to get a menu.[13] Click on Hyperlink on this menu. Click on the Bookmarks button and then select the desired bookmark by clicking on it, then click OK. The desired bookmark in this case is *EXPERIENCEofPRESERVED*, the same bookmark we inserted in the *Person* number field of the child line for Experience in her parents' sketch. That is all there is to it! You can now press Control + Click on EXPERIENCE[2] PARTRIDGE in your document to be carried back to line ii of Preserved's sketch. Notice that the WORD cursor changes to a pointing finger when you pass over a "hot" name, one that has a hyperlink in it.

After we learn how to hyperlink in the other direction, I will show you how to get rid of the need to press Control, so that just a click will carry you to the remote location. And we will deal with the underline and colored text problem.

Let's do the other half of hyperlinking first. Let's establish a hyperlink to get from the child list to the corresponding sketch for that child. First, insert a new bookmark in the child's sketch. For example, in the sketch for Experience Partridge, click in a convenient place for a bookmark, say just left of Experience's name. Then, using the insert bookmark skill, insert a bookmark there with a memorable name. I suggest using something like *EXPERIENCEofPRESERVED_down*. Notice that this is the same name that takes us up, from child sketch to parent sketch, but with the suffix *_down* to remind us that it is for the corresponding hyperlink in the opposite direction, down from parent to child. Now return to the child item under Preserved. This is easy! Just Control + Click on the hyperlink you've already established. Then select EXPERIENCE PARTRIDGE (select the whole name) on line ii and insert the hyperlink to the bookmark you've just created. You can, as before, right click-on her name,[14] click on Hyperlink: Bookmark: *EXPERIENCEofPRESERVED_down:* OK: OK *(Figs. 12–13).* Or you can

---

[13] If this right-click menu in your version of WORD does not have the Hyperlink command, then you will have to use the alternative approach: click on Insert: Hyperlink. If you have a Mac, Control + Click is the equivalent of right-click.

[14] If your version of WORD allows it.

click on Insert: Hyperlink: Bookmark:*EXPERIENCEofPRESERVED_down:* OK: OK *(Fig. 14).* That's it. You can now leap back and forth between parent and child.

I recommend that you insert these hyperlinks, in both directions, as you generate each child's sketch. You will find them immediately helpful (as we did above).

You will have noticed that two bookmarks are needed for each

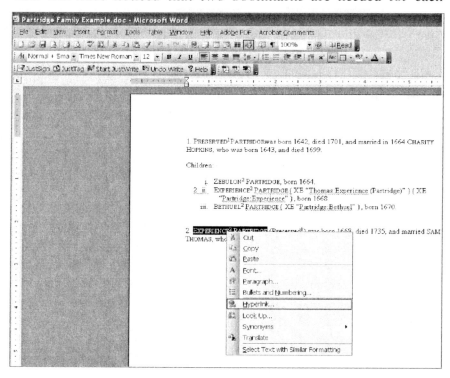

Fig. 12. Right-click on EXPERIENCE PARTRIDGE
and click on **Hyperlink.**

sketch, except the first. You do not have to use the bookmark-naming conventions I have used in the examples, but it is important to use some scheme that is consistent, so that you don't get confused. The scheme suggested above has the advantage of requiring invention of only one unique name per sketch rather than two.

Fig. 13. Click on Bookmark:
EXPERIENCEofPRESERVED_down: OK: OK.

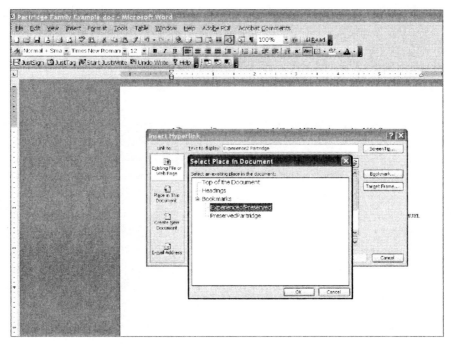

Fig. 14. Select
EXPERIENCEofPRESERVED_down: OK: OK.

Now, as promised, let's learn how to get rid of the need to press both Control *and* Click to make a hyperlink. To do this: Click on Tools: Options: Edit and turn off the checkmark by Use Control + Click to follow hyperlink. Then click OK (Fig 15). Now just a click will transfer you through the document. You will note that when you hover over a word containing a hyperlink, a message comes up telling you to Click to follow link. This is how you can tell a hyperlink is embedded.

Next problem: You have undoubtedly noticed WORD's default tendency to underline text that contains a hyperlink and turn it some color, like blue or magenta. This is well-known behavior for web pages but is not useful in a genealogical document not meant for the web. Recall that the hyperlinks internal to a genealogical document are for the author's use, not for the reader's. In general, we want these hyperlinks to be invisible to the reader. The blue or magenta

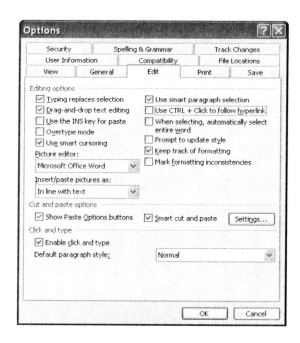

Fig. 15. Click on Tools: Options: Edit *and turn off the checkmark by* Use Control + Click to follow hyperlink. *Then click* OK.

underlined words *are* visible exactly that way in a printed WORD document, so next we will see how to get rid of the underline and the color while maintaining the hyperlink.

Unfortunately, "versionitis" is a serious problem on this topic, so if you have an older version of WORD, be sure to read the paragraphs below that are surrounded with square brackets. They will instruct you on alternatives that are required in older versions. In either case, read the immediately following paragraph:

You need to change the formatting that WORD automatically applies to hyperlinks. To do this, click on Format: Styles and Formatting. This causes display of a list of the formats built into WORD. The ones to change are called Hyperlink and FollowedHyperlink. Find the item Hyperlink on the list. As you hover over the item, a down arrow will display to the right of the item. Click on this down arrow, then click on Modify. Click on the button labeled U to turn underlining off. Click on the down arrow next to the button labeled with an A and a bar of color (probably blue or magenta). This will cause display of a color palette. Select a square colored black. If the box labeled Formatting is not empty, delete what is there.[15] If the box next to it, for font size, is not empty, delete what is there.[16] IMPORTANT — Turn on the checkmark beside Add to Template by clicking on the little box there, and click OK. Then save your file. This will store the new Hyperlink format. Repeat the above for the style FollowedHyperlink, which is the style used once you have used a link to make an actual jump. This may seem like a lot of work, but once it's done, it never has to be revisited.

[For older versions of WORD: You will be dismayed to see your careful choices of font and font size blown away by the procedure above. Also your choices of case (italic, bold, small caps, etc.) are destroyed, and if you had a generation superscript in the name, it is lost. This is because older versions of WORD associate a specific font,

---

[15] Older versions of WORD don't allow you to delete the font name here. Just proceed to the next step. We will fix this in the bracketed paragraphs below.

[16] See note 6.

font size, etc. with a hyperlink. One of the improvements offered by newer versions is the ability to preserve the font characteristics of a hyperlinked word, whatever they are. There is a workaround for this flaw, but it is cumbersome. Nevertheless, users agree that the resulting power of hyperlinks is worth the effort. So here goes:]

[It *is* possible to change the formatting of a hyperlinked word or words after you have inserted the hyperlink. To do this you must select the word (or words) and set the format in the usual way with Format: Font or with toolbar commands. But there is a problem. If you click on a word with a hyperlink embedded in it, you will cause a leap to the target location, and not be able to select the word. So how do you select the word for reformatting? There is a trick you can use: Select near the word, but not on the word, and then use the arrow keys to step into the word. If you also hold down the Shift key while moving the cursor with an arrow key, you can select the desired word.]

[Other tips to consider in this situation are these: To simplify the reformatting task, choose only, say, the first name to make "hot" with a hyperlink. The idea here is to reduce the amount of reformatting required by, for example, not including a superscript. Another idea is to make a space near a name "hot," rather than the name itself. With this idea you won't even have to reformat. A third idea is to embed hyperlinks in words of a constant format. In this case, you can set the single set of parameters in the Modify dialog box used to modify the Hyperlink and FollowedHyperlink styles. But this tip requires that the format of all words with embedded hyperlinks must be identical in font, size, and case.]

Updating existing documents

These instructions should be read in conjunction with the preceding instructions of the same name, in the section about automatic numbering and renumbering. In step 3 there, the insertion of automatic sketch numbers, I suggested that hyperlinks are conveniently inserted during that step:

1. Insert a hyperlink from each child line with a sketch expansion to the corresponding sketch and a hyperlink back to the correspon-

ding child line. For maximum efficiency, click at the left of the name at the beginning of a sketch (except the first), insert a new bookmark that is related in a systematic way with the bookmark that you used to automatically number the sketch. Suppose that bookmark were named *EXPERIENCEofPRESERVED*, then the new bookmark might be named *EXPERIENCEofPRESERVED_down*, since it will be used, in step 4, to pass down the family tree from the parent sketch to this child sketch.

2. Then select the person's name for this sketch and insert a hyperlink there to the original bookmark. Insert: Hyperlink: Bookmark: *EXPERIENCEofPRESERVED*: OK: OK will do it (or right-click then Hyperlink: Bookmark: *EXPERIENCEofPRESERVED*: OK: OK for some versions of WORD), for example.[17]

3. Now execute the hyperlink you just embedded in step 2, which should take you to the corresponding child line in the parents' sketch.

4. Insert the new hyperlink you created in step 1 here: Select the child's name and Insert: Hyperlink: Bookmark: *EXPERIENCEof PRESERVED_down*: OK: OK (or right-click then Hyperlink: Bookmark: *EXPERIENCEofPRESERVED*: OK: OK), for example.[18]

5. Execute the hyperlink you just embedded in step 4, which should take you back to the child's sketch where you started in step 1. This step serves as a check that you can jump both up and down the tree properly.

6. Repeat steps 1–5 for each child sketch in the paper. Notice that at the end of step 5 you are in easy position to find the next sketch and start again with step 1 above.

N.B.: If you find that you need to change the hyperlink in a word or words that already has one, it is a good idea to delete the hyperlink that is there first. This is easy: right-click on the word or words with the hyperlink and click on Delete Hyperlink.

---

[17] For older versions of WORD, here you might also have to reformat the words or words with embedded hyperlink.

[18] See note 8.

AUTOMATIC TABLE GENERATION

Before describing the basics of automatic tables, let's review another fundamental WORD skill that is required, the Show All skill.

The techniques described here will always require that the author be utilizing the view mode in WORD known as Show All, which explicitly shows all paragraphs, spaces, and tabs you have inserted in the document, and much more, as we shall see.

To view a document in Show All mode, click on Tools on the main menu bar, click on Options, click on View, click on the box next to All, under Formatting marks, so that a checkmark appears. As before this process can be abbreviated to: click on Tools: Options: View: All. To Hide All, do exactly the same sequence, but turn off the checkmark by All.

A quick way to do this is simply to click on the toolbar button showing the paragraph symbol, ¶. Successive clicks on this button toggle between Show All and Hide All.[19]

Toggling between Show All and Hide All should be second nature to you because it will be used often. From hereon I will simply instruct you to Show All or Hide All, without further elaboration.

The basic idea for generating automatic tables is: (1) tag items to be entered automatically in a table; (2) insert the table where you want it to appear; and (3) cause the table to be automatically generated at the desired location, showing tagged items and page numbers on which they appear. You never have to know the page numbers yourself; this task is taken care of automatically by WORD.

The techniques described here can be used to generate a table of contents, a table of illustrations, a name index, a place index, and so forth. We will start with a simple name index.

To accomplish this task, we shall first tag each name as it is entered into our document. This explanation assumes you are viewing your document in Show All mode.

---

[19] If your toolbar does not have such a button, you may place one there by clicking on Tools: Options: Customize: View. Find the paragraph symbol in the list. Drag and drop it onto your toolbar.

Tagging would be a torturous job should you wait until the last minute and try to do it at one pass. By far the best policy is to do it is as you go. That is, every time you enter a name to be indexed, tag it then. Here is how to accomplish the WORD tagging skill.

Click just left of a name you wish to tag for your name index. Here's an easy way to do it: Click Shift + Alt + X *(Fig. 16)*. That is, type all three keys at the same time. This procedure opens up a dialog box. You may then enter a surname in the top box, and a first name or names in the second box. Then click Mark. A tag field that looks like { XE "Doe:John" } is generated next to the name you are indexing.[20]

The dialog box stays open so that you can tag several names. To tag another name, you must click twice. The first click changes focus

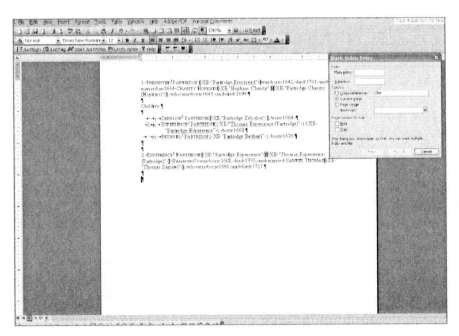

Fig. 16. Click Shift + Alt + X. *That is, type all three keys at the same time. You may then enter a surname in the top box, and a first name or names in the second box.*

---

[20] There is a difficult way also: click on Insert: Field: XE and then type in the name in the format required—for example, "Doe:John", where *the quotation marks are required.*

from the dialog box to the text document. The second click actually indicates where you want the next tag to appear. Then click on the dialog box to bring focus back to it, and proceed as before.

Example 9. Let's index our running example. Again there is no need to construct a separate Modified *Register* [NGSQ] format example, since precisely the same technique works in either case. The item below is presented as you would see it in Show All mode — except I have not bothered to show all the space, tab, and paragraph marks that would actually be displayed in this mode, since these marks would obscure the main message I am trying to convey. All items are tagged using the tagging skill just explained.

1. PRESERVED[1] PARTRIDGE{ XE "Partridge:Preserved" } was born 1642, died 1701, and married in 1664 CHARITY HOPKINS{ XE "Partridge:Charity (Hopkins) } { XE "Hopkins:Charity" }, who was born 1643, and died 1699.

Children:

    i. ZEBULON[2] PARTRIDGE{ XE "Partridge:Zebulon" }, born 1664.

2. ii. EXPERIENCE PARTRIDGE{ XE "Thomas:Experience (Partridge)" }{ XE "Partridge:Experience" }, born 1668.

    iii. BETHUEL PARTRIDGE{ XE "Partridge:Bethuel" }, born 1670.

2. EXPERIENCE[2] PARTRIDGE{ XE "Thomas:Experience (Partridge)" }{ XE "Partridge: Experience" }(*Preserved*[1]) was born 1668, died 1735, and married SAMUEL THOMAS { XE "Thomas:Samuel" }, who was born 1666, and died 1727.

IMPORTANT — The index tags for the same person in two different places must be *exactly* the same. For example, { XE "Partridge:Experience" } in one place but { XE "Partridge:Experience " } in the other would produce two different entries in the name index, although they would appear to you as a duplicate entry. Do you see why? There is an extra space after Experience's given name in the second instance. WORD's indexing system would assume you meant two different people.

The only surprise in the example sketches above might be the second tags before Charity and Experience. It is typical in a name index to list women under both their maiden and married names. The second tags are to generate an index item for these two women under their married names. In these tag fields, the name to the left of the colon is the married surname, and to the right of the colon is the woman's maiden name, with her maiden surname in parentheses.

Suppose Experience married a second time to William Twitchell. Then a third tag would be prepended to her name, looking like this { XE "Twitchell:Experience (Partridge) (Thomas)" }.

You will notice that tagging clutters up your document. The example above does not convey just how messy **Show All** can be, since I have not shown the space, tab, and paragraph marks. To see your document as others will see it, and to return yourself to sanity, simply **Hide All**.

Now we need to learn the skill of inserting an actual index table into the document. Although complicated, once done, this task never has to be repeated — unless you want to change the formatting.

Click on the place in your document where you want the name index to appear. For example, you might want to choose the very end of your document.

It probably goes without saying, but let's be explicit. Since you are going to show page numbers in the name index, it only makes sense to have page numbers showing on your pages. I will assume you know how to insert page numbers into a footer or a header for each page.

At the desired location for the name index, do the following: Click on **Insert: Field: Index**. To find **Index** in the list more easily, you might want to click first on the **Index and Tables** item under **Categories**. Then click on the button labeled **Index** *(Fig. 17)*. Before clicking **OK**, consider the following:

I recommend the following choice of options in the dialog box to get started: leave unchecked the box next to **Right align page numbers**;

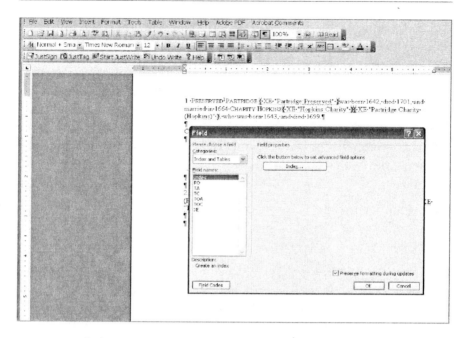

Fig. 17. Click on Insert: Field: Index. *To find* Index *in the list more easily, you might want to click first on the* Index and Tables *item under* Categories. *Then click on the button labeled* Index.

set Formats to From templates; set Type to Indented; set Columns to 1; set Language to English (U.S.) *(Fig. 18)*; click on the button Modify and note that the formats listed there are Index 1, Index 2, etc. *(Fig. 19)*. For now, I suggest using the default settings of these formats, but return here later to modify these formats. Click Cancel to exit the Modify dialog. Click OK to enter your name index table.

There are lots of variations on an index you might want to make. For example, for longer documents you will almost surely want two columns (or more) rather than one. You might want surnames listed in a different format from given names under it. I will save these formatting matters for a future installment. First let's master the basics.

Example 10. Let's assume that you have entered the name index field code at the end of your document, as just suggested. Let's further assume that, for whatever reason, the sketch for Preserved Partridge appears on page 5 and that for Experience on page 49. In general, we

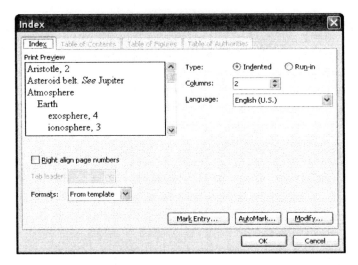

Fig. 18. *Leave the box next to* Right align page numbers
unchecked; set Formats *to* From templates; *set* Type *to* Indented;
set Columns *to* 1; *set* Language *to* English (U.S.).

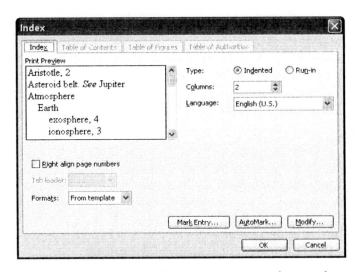

Fig. 19. *Click on the button* Modify *and note that*
the formats listed there are Index 1, Index 2, *etc.*

don't know what the actual page numbers are; WORD figures this out for us. When you click on OK, after the index table field code insertion, you will immediately see the following at the desired location. I am assuming a one-column table in indented format.

Hopkins
    Charity, 5

Partridge
    Bethuel, 5
    Charity (Hopkins), 5
    Experience, 5, 49
    Preserved, 5
    Zebulon, 5

Thomas
    Experience (Partridge), 5, 49
    Samuel, 49

Updating an Index. Now the final skill to learn is how to update an index that is already in place. Suppose twenty new persons have been added to your document, complete with index tags, since last you generated an index. To update the document, including the index, do the following:

1. Set **Hide All** mode.

2. Apply **Select All** to the document. One way to do this is to click on **Edit:Select All**. Another way is to click on your main document text somewhere. It doesn't matter where so long as it falls in the main body of text — the title page is a good place to click. Then type **Control + A.**

3. Click on the **F9** key. If a dialog box appears asking you to make a choice between simply updating the page numbers in a table or updating the entire table, select the second option: **Update entire table,** and click OK. This might take a while to execute in large documents, since you've just asked WORD to do a lot of work.

4. Save your file.

Something I have glossed over until now is formatting an index. Let's revisit that topic. It is not difficult. Recall that I already showed you where to find the formatting styles called Index 1, Index 2, Index 3, and so forth that WORD uses for formatting indexes. Index 1 is for the first field, surnames in this case. Index 2 is for the second field, given names in this case. And so forth.

Here's how to modify one of these formatting styles: Click on Insert: Field: Index: Index: Modify: Index 1: Modify *(Fig. 20)*. This will open up a dialog box to allow you to set the format attached to style Index 1. You can choose bold or italic, for example. You can raise or lower the font size. You can change the type face. You can change the spacing before or after the line. And so forth. Before you click OK, do the following: Click on the box next to Add to template to turn on the checkmark there. Be sure that there is a checkmark in the box next to Automatic update. Now click OK. You might elect to repeat this procedure for Index 2. Now when you click on OK for the Index dialog box, the index generated will use the new formats.

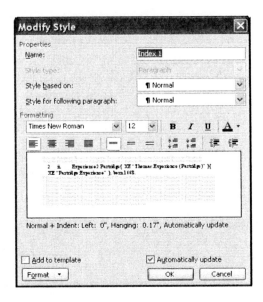

Fig. 20. To modify formatting styles: Click on
Insert: Field: Index: Index: Modify: Index 1: Modify.

Example 11. Delete the index previously generated and click where you want to insert a new one. This time we will modify **Index 1** and **Index 2** and use two columns. I set **Index 1** to boldface but made no further changes. I set **Index 2** to a smaller font size and tightened the spacing between lines. I set the number of columns to 2. And here is the new name index using these new settings:

Hopkins
  Charity, 5

Partridge
  Bethuel, 5
  Charity (Hopkins), 5
  Experience, 5, 49

Preserved, 5
Zebulon, 5

Thomas
Experience
  (Partridge), 5, 49
Samuel, 49

Now let's generate a table of contents to demonstrate how the same skills used for indexes work for this task too. We enter a slightly different tag for a table of contents and a slightly different field code where the table is to actually reside in the document. Other than that, the same steps as above apply: (1) Insert tags; (2) insert table; and (3) update the table.

The tag to be inserted is obtained by **Insert: Field: TC**. Then you insert the text you want to show in the table of contents in the box provided. Before closing this dialog box, note the checkbox labeled **Outline level**. If you check this box, then you should enter a digit in the box to its right. If you enter a 1 then formatting style **TOC 1** will be used. If you enter a 2 then **TOC 2** will be used. And so forth. We will use the default table of contents form first, where the **Outline level** box is left unchecked, which defaults formatting to **TOC 1**. Then click **OK** to enter the table of contents tag.

Example 12. A good way to demonstrate table of contents tagging is by example, using our running example. What is shown here is the document as seen in **Show All** mode, sans the space, tab, and paragraph marks as before. The idea in this example is to enter each sketch into our table of contents. To that end we have inserted the TC tags in two places as just described. The XE index tags will show too, of course.

1. { TC "1. Partridge:Preserved" }PRESERVED[1]PARTRIDGE
{ XE "Partridge:Preserved" }was born 1642, died 1701,
and married in 1664 CHARITY HOPKINS{ XE "Partridge:
Charity (Hopkins) }{ XE "Hopkins:Charity" }, who was
born 1643, and died 1699.

   Children:
        i.   ZEBULON[2] PARTRIDGE{ XE "Partridge:Zebulon" },
             born 1664.
   2.   ii. EXPERIENCE PARTRIDGE{ XE "Thomas:Experience
             (Partridge)" }{ XE "Partridge:Experience" }, born
             1668.
        iii. BETHUEL PARTRIDGE{ XE "Partridge:Bethuel" },
             born 1670.

. . . [Assume many pages here to make this example meaningful.]

   2. { TC ". Experience Partridge" }EXPERIENCE[2] PARTRIDGE
   { XE "Thomas:Experience (Partridge)" }{ XE "Partridge:
   Experience" }(*Preserved[1]*) was born 1668, died 1735, and
   married SAMUEL THOMAS{ XE "Thomas:Samuel" }, who
   was born 1666, and died 1727.

VERY IMPORTANT: The numbers in the two TC tags are automatic numbers, not explicit ones. Otherwise the whole idea of automatic numbering is defeated. To accomplish this kind of numbering, the
same field entered for the number at the beginning of the sketch is
entered in the TC number postion too. Recall that the field you
inserted as the number field of the sketch is of the form SEQ Person
[*bookmarkname*]. For the number field in the TC field code, you
want exactly the same construct. The easiest way to ensure this construct is to select the number field at the beginning of the sketch,
then copy and paste it (with Control + C and then Control + V) into
the number field position of the TC field code. You can, of course,
go through the pain of actually entering the same SEQ Person [*bookmarkname*] number field, if you want to.

I usually enter the sketch number field and the TC tag at the same
time when I am writing a paper. I usually get this part of a sketch
from one that I have already entered, with a copy and paste, then I

change the name of the person. I then enter the SEQ Person [*book-markname*] field into either the sketch number. Then here's a trick: Use F4 to repeat the last step exactly. In other words, IMMEDIATE-LY after I do the automatic number field insert, I select the TC number field and type F4. This key causes the identical number field to be embedded into the second place. This step only works if it is immediately the next thing you do. Remember to select the line and type F9 to update the fields (or play it safe and Select All and F9).

As before, Hide All hides all the ugly tag fields and reveals what a reader will see.

Now let's enter the actual table of contents in a convenient location, say, just after the title. Click there, click on Insert: Field: TOC, and then click on the button labeled Table of Contents *(Fig. 21)*. There are several formatting decisions to make.

I suggest the following as a starting point: Turn on Show page numbers, Right align page numbers, and select the dotted line for Page

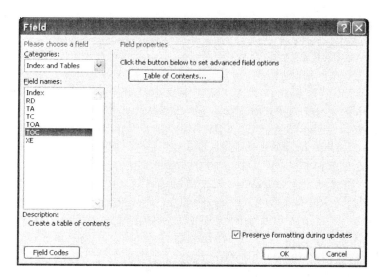

Fig. 21. Click on Insert: Field: TOC, *and then click on the button labeled* Table of Contents.

leader. Set Formats to From template. Set Show levels to 3. Check the box next to Use hyperlinks instead of page numbers *(Fig. 22)*. This one is an important setting, but ineptly named. What this setting does is turn on hyperlinks in your table of contents, which is very convenient. The "instead of page numbers" is merely confusing. Click on the box named Options and in the dialog box there turn on a checkmark next to Table entry fields and turn off all others, then click OK. This procedure returns you to the table of contents dialog box. Before clicking on OK here, consider the following:

Just as you did for indexes, click on the button labeled Modify. A dialog box is opened that lists the default formatting styles used by WORD for tables of contents. We will not modify these styles now, but note that TOC 1 will be used by default or for TC tag fields that include the switch \l 1. TOC 2 will be used for items tagged with \l 2 in the TC field. And so forth. For now, click Cancel, then click OK in the table of contents dialog box to cause your table to be generated in the place first indicated.

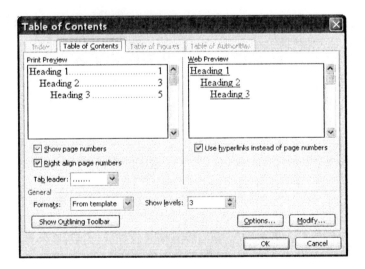

Fig. 22. Turn on Show page numbers, Right align page numbers, *and select the dotted line for* Page leader. *Set* Formats *to* From template. *Set* Show levels *to* 3. *Check the box next to* Use hyperlinks instead of page numbers.

Example 13. Let's again assume that, for whatever reason, the sketch for Preserved Partridge appears on page 5 and that for Experience on page 49. When you click on **OK**, after the table of contents field code insertion described just above, you will immediately see the following at the desired location. I am assuming the formatting choices just recommended.

1.   Preserved Partridge   5
2.   Experience Partridge   49

N.B.: This table of contents is "hot." That is, WORD automatically inserts hyperlinks from items in an automatically generated table of contents to the corresponding page. So a click on the second line above would take you directly to page 49 and Experience's sketch. Remember **Use hyperlinks instead of page numbers?** This is the checkbox that made your table "hot."

To update a table of contents after additions have been made, follow exactly the same updating procedure as described above for indexes: **Hide All. Select All. F9.** Choose the **Update entire table** option, if offered, then click **OK**. Save the file.

A word of caution: Do not attempt to edit an automatically generated table. You *can* edit one without a problem, but all edits will be lost the next time you do an automatic update. The only time it makes sense to edit such a table is immediately prior to publication when you know there are no further changes.

For the final example I will show you how to modify the formatting of a table of contents. You have probably already guessed how to do it.

Example 14. Assume that the tag fields for the two sketches above are changed to { TC ". Partridge:Preserved" \l 2 } and { TC ". Experience: Preserved" \l 2 }. Furthermore, assume that we introduced two subtitles in the document. One, before the sketches, being the following:

{ TC "Sketches" \l 1 }SKETCHES

and the other, before the name index, being this:

{ TC "Sketches" \l 1 }NAME INDEX

Notice that I have explicitly entered the "level" option \l1 or \l2 into these commands, which will cause WORD to use TOC 1 or TOC 2, respectively, to format the corresponding items. Then an update of the document would generate the following table of contents, where I have implicitly modified TOC 1 and TOC 2 to cause the following display:

There is one further item worth mentioning before closing: Named automatic tables. These tables are similar to named sequences of automatic numbers. The purpose is also similar: to allow the mixture of several tables in the same document while keeping their identities separate.

For example, suppose that you want a place index as well as a name index. This task is accomplished by inserting into each index tag a name field, such as \f *"Place"*, to indicate that the corresponding item is to go into the index table that is named *Place*. Thus an index tag inserted next to Boston in the text might look like this:

{ XE "Massachusetts:Boston" \f "Place" }

Then the Index field for the table itself must also have this \f *"Place"* option specified, *where the quotation marks are required*. You would enter a table such as this as follows: Click on Insert: Field: Index: Field Codes, and then explicitly typing in \f *"Place"* in the box provided, then click OK *(Fig. 23)*.

Similarly, suppose that you want a table of illustrations as well as a table of contents. In this case you don't have to explicitly label the tagged items since WORD performs this task for you, but you do have to know to insert the option \f Figure in the TOC field used to generate the actual table of illustrations.

Finally, to see these field codes explicitly, and assuming you are really brave or just must edit them by hand, then do the following: Select the area whose field codes you want to see. Click on Tools:

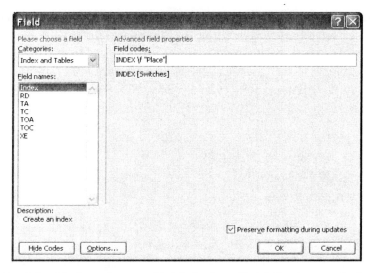

Fig. 23. Click on Insert: Field: Index: Field Codes, *and then explicitly type in* \f "Place" *in the box provided, then click* OK.

Options: View: Field code (under Show): OK. Uncheck the same box to return to normal view *(Fig. 24).*[21]

I can promise you that after a little while with these techniques, they become second nature, and greatly increase the flexibility of your genealogy document.

You won't be able to imagine how you lived without them, especially the hyperlinking and the automatic renumbering.

---

[21] If you find yourself performing this task often, you might want to put a button for it in your toolbar: Click on Tools: Customize: View: View Field Codes. Drag and drop this last item onto your toolbar. It is a button labeled with {a}.

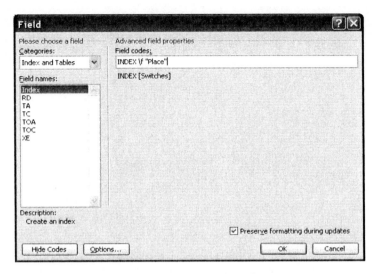

Fig. 24. Select the area whose field codes you want to see.
Click on **Tools: Options: View: Field code (under Show): OK.**
Uncheck the same box to return to normal view.

APPENDIX A
Abbreviations and Acronyms

This list is intended to help readers interpret the many abbreviations and acronyms used in American genealogy now and in the past. Several of these abbreviations are no longer in use and/or are not recommended. Two journals, *National Genealogical Society Quarterly* and *Pennsylvania Genealogical Magazine*, now use practically no abbreviations.

Some abbreviations may appear with an initial capital letter, depending on the context. Some Latin words and abbreviations may or may not be italicized. Some letter abbreviations and acronyms appear with or without periods. A few appear only without periods (e.g., DAR) and a few appear only with periods (e.g., O.S.). For acronyms, it is good practice to write out the name in full at first use, followed by the acronym in brackets.

adm./admin.	administration
admr.	administrator
ae.	aged [*aetatis*]
AG	Accredited Genealogist*
AGBI	*American Genealogical-Biographical Index*
APG	Association of Professional Genealogists
b.	born
BCG	Board for Certification of Genealogists†
bp./bap.	baptized
bur.	buried
ca./c.	about [*circa*]
CAILS	Certified American Indian Lineage Specialist†
calc.	calculated

CALS	Certified American Lineage Specialist†
cem.	cemetery
CG	Certified Genealogist†
CG(C)	Certified Genealogist (Canada)‡
CGI	Certified Genealogical Instructor†
CGL	Certified Genealogical Lecturer†
CGRS	Certified Genealogical Record Searcher†
ch.	children; church
chr.	christened
CLS	Certified Lineage Specialist†
co.	county
col.	column; colony; colonial
coll(s).	collection(s)
comm.	committee
comp.	compiler
ct.	court
d.	died
DAR	Daughters of the American Revolution
dau.	daughter
decd.	deceased
dist.	district
div.	divorced
d.s.p.	died without issue [*sine prole*]
d.y.	died young
ed.	edited by; editor; edition
ED	Enumeration District; Election District
exec.	executor
f./fo./fol.	folio
FASG	Fellow of the American Society of Genealogists
ff.	and following pages
FGS	Federation of Genealogical Societies
FHL	Family History Library
fl.	alive during [*floruit*, "flourished"]

fn.	footnote
FUGA	Fellow of the Utah Genealogical Association
gen.	genealogical; genealogy; generation
GPC	Genealogical Publishing Co.
GRS(C)	Genealogical Record Searcher (Canada)‡
g.s.	gravestone
hist.	historical; history
ibid.	same as the preceding citation [short for *ibidem,* "in the same place"]
IGI	International Genealogical Index
inst.	instant [in the current month]
int.	intention [marriage intention]
inv.	inventory
LAC	Library and Archives Canada
LC	Library of Congress [see LOC]
LDS	The Church of Jesus Christ of Latter-day Saints
lic.	license
LOC	Library of Congress [see LC]
LR	land records/deeds
£-s-d	pounds, shillings, pence
m/mo.	month [in Quaker dates]
m.	married
MD	*The Mayflower Descendant*
MQ	*The Mayflower Quarterly*
MS./ms.	manuscript
MSS./mss.	manuscripts
n./nn.	note(s) [as in footnote(s)]
NA	National Archives (Canada)
NARA	National Archives and Records Administration (U.S.)
N.B.	*nota bene* ("note well")
n.d.	no publication date
NEA	*New England Ancestors* magazine
NEHGR	*The New England Historical and Genealogical Register* [see *Register*]

NEHGS	New England Historic Genealogical Society
NGS	National Genealogical Society
NGSQ	*National Genealogical Society Quarterly*
NHGR	*The New Hampshire Genealogical Record*
no.	number
n.p.	no place; no publisher
n.s.	new series
N.S.	New Style [date]
NSDAR	National Society, Daughters of the American Revolution
NYGBR	*The New York Genealogical and Biographical Record* [see *Record*]
obit.	obituary
o.s.	old series
O.S.	Old Style [date]
p./pp.	page(s)
passim	at various places in a cited portion of text [*passim*, "here and there"]
PCC	Prerogative Court of Canterbury
PERSI	*Periodical Source Index*
PGM	*The Pennsylvania Genealogical Magazine*
PR	probate records
PRO	Public Record Office [see TNA]
pt.	part
pub(s).	published; publication(s)
r	*recto* [on the front of the page or the right-hand page]
rec(s).	record(s)
Record	*The New York Genealogical and Biographical Record* [see NYGBR] or *The New Hampshire Genealogical Record* [see NHGR]
Register	*The New England Historical and Genealogical Register* [see NEHGR]
rem.	removed
repr./rpt.	reprint(ed)
res.	resided
rev. ed.	revised edition

Rev War	Revolutionary War
RG	Record Group
SAR	Sons of the American Revolution
ser.	series
sic	thus [indicates a word misspelled or wrongly used in the original]
Soc.	Society
supp.	supplement
supra	above
TAG	*The American Genealogist*
TEG	*The Essex Genealogist*
TG	*The Genealogist*
TNA	The National Archives of England, Wales, and the United Kingdom [formerly PRO]
TR	town records
trans./transl.	translated by; translator
transcr.	transcribed by; transcriber
TS./TSS.	typescript(s)
twp.	township
ult.	*ultimo* [in the preceding month]
unk.	unknown
unm.	unmarried
unpub.	unpublished
v	*verso* [on the back of the page or the left-hand page]
v./vs.	versus
var.	variant
viz.	namely [*videlicet*, "it can be seen"]
vol(s).	volume(s)
VR	vital records
w.	wife, widow
w.d.	will dated
wid.	widow
w.p.	will proved
y-m-d	years, months, days [for age at death]

*AG identifies genealogists who meet competency standards of the International Commission for the Accreditation of Professional Genealogists.

†CG, CGI, and CGL are service marks of the Board for Certification of Genealogists®, used under license by associates who meet genealogical competency standards prescribed for its particular programs. CGRS, CALS, CAILS, and CLS are no longer used by the Board.

‡CG(C) and GRS(C) identify genealogists who meet competency standards of the Genealogical Institute of the Maritimes.

APPENDIX B

Commonly Used Symbols

Compiled genealogies often use symbols instead of words. Below are a number of common symbols used in the field. Some (such as &c.) may be used with or without a period.

[ ]	insertion of missing text; text in original record missing or illegible
~	circa; about; approximately; when used above or through a letter, it indicates the omission of one or more letters or syllables (e.g., appur̃ces = appurtenances)
. . .	ellipsis (precedes or follows a partial quote of a sentence indicating additional words in the original, with four ellipsis points indicating the end of a sentence); some transcribers use the ellipsis to indicate illegible material
+	indicates family carried forward in a compiled genealogy
?	uncertain interpretation of original text
>	after, more than
<	before, less than
#	number; pound
$/dol	dollar
¢/c/ct	cent
£	pound sterling
s	shilling
d	penny, pence
y	thorn, Anglo Saxon character for the sound *th* (e.g., *ye* = the)

g	character sometimes used to represent the *th* sound in *worth*
&	and
&c./etc.	*et cetera* ["and so forth"]
& al.	*et alii, et alios, et aliis* ["and others"]
& ux.	*et uxor* ["and wife"]
"	ditto (same as above); inch
'	foot
—-	information is missing
*, †, ‡	symbols often used to indicate footnote
*	born (especially in European works)
∞	married (especially in European works)
†	died
:	part of word omitted (e.g., *Will:* = William)
x^2	superscript numbers (i.e., ^{1}, ^{2}, ^{3}, etc.) indicate generation of descent from the immigrant ancestor; superscript letters (i.e., ^{A}, ^{B}, ^{C}, etc.) show generations of ascent from the immigrant ancestor; superscript letters show that part of the word is left out (e.g., *Thos* = Thomas)
‾	overline, used over a letter to indicate the omission of *m* or *n* as the following letter (e.g., *com̅on*)
/	indicates alternate reading of words (e.g., Edmund/Edward)
-	hyphen; joins two words into one
–	en dash; expresses a range of numbers or years
—	em dash; signifies a major break in thought

Geographical Abbreviations

The standard for U.S. state and Canadian provincial abbreviations in genealogical publishing is to use the old-style, long-form abbreviations, not the modern two-letter postal abbreviation.

U.S. STATES

Alabama	Ala.	Louisiana	La.
Alaska	Alas. or Ak.	Maine	Me.
Arizona	Ariz.	Maryland	Md.
Arkansas	Ark.	Massachusetts	Mass.
California	Cal. or Calif.	Michigan	Mich.
Colorado	Col. or Colo.	Minnesota	Minn.
Connecticut	Conn.	Mississippi	Miss.
Delaware	Del.	Missouri	Mo.
Florida	Fla.	Montana	Mont.
Georgia	Ga.	Nebraska	Neb. or Nebr.
Hawaii	(none)	Nevada	Nev.
Idaho	Ida.	New Hampshire	N.H.
Illinois	Ill.	New Jersey	N.J.
Indiana	Ind.	New Mexico	N.Mex.
Iowa	Ia.	New York	N.Y.
Kansas	Kans.	North Carolina	N.C.
Kentucky	Ky.	North Dakota	N.Dak.

U.S. STATES CONTINUED

Ohio	O.	Texas	Tex.
Oklahoma	Okla.	Utah	Ut.
Oregon	Ore. or Oreg.	Vermont	Vt.
Pennsylvania	Pa. or Penn. or Penna.	Virginia	Va. or Vir.
		Washington	Wash.
Rhode Island	R.I.	West Virginia	W.Va. or W.Vir.
South Carolina	S.C.		
South Dakota	S.Dak.	Wisconsin	Wis. or Wisc.
Tennessee	Tenn.	Wyoming	Wyo.

CANADIAN PROVINCES

Alberta	Alta.
British Columbia	B.C.
Manitoba	Man.
New Brunswick	N.B.
Newfoundland	Nfld.
Nova Scotia	N.S.
Northwest Territories	N.W.T.
Ontario	Ont.
Prince Edward Island	P.E.I.
Quebec	Que.
Saskatchewan	Sask.
Yukon Territory	Yuk. or Y.T.

BIBLIOGRAPHY

37Signals. *Defensive Design for the Web: How to Improve Error Messages, Help, Forms, and Other Crisis Points* (Indianapolis, Ind.: New Riders, 2006).

Board for Certification of Genealogists. *The BCG Genealogical Standards Manual* (Orem, Utah: Ancestry Publishing, 2000).

Bunnin, Brad, and Peter Beren. *The Writer's Legal Companion* (New York: Perseus Books, 1999).

Carmack, Sharon DeBartolo. *Carmack's Guide to Copyright and Contracts: A Primer for Genealogists, Writers & Researchers* (Baltimore: Genealogical Publishing Company, 2005).

Chappon, Rene J., ed. *The Associated Press Guide to Punctuation* (Cambridge, Mass.: Perseus Publishing, 2003).

The Chicago Manual of Style, 15th ed. (Chicago: University of Chicago Press, 2003).

Costello, Margaret F., and Jane Fletcher Fiske. *Guidelines for Genealogical Writing: Style Guide for* The New England Historical and Genealogical Register *with Suggestions for Genealogical Books* (Boston: NEHGS, 1990).

Curran, Joan Ferris; Madilyn Coen Crane; and John H. Wray. *Numbering Your Genealogy: Basic Systems, Complex Families, and International Kin*, National Genealogical Society Special Publication No. 64 (Arlington, Va.: National Genealogical Society, 2000).

Fryxell, David. *How to Write Fast (While Writing Well): A Guide to Speed, Organization, Concentration, Problem-Solving, and Creativity* (Cincinnati: Writer's Digest Books, 1992).

Hatcher, Patricia Law. *Producing a Quality Family History* (Salt Lake City: Ancestry, 1996).

Kozachek, Thomas. *Guidelines for Authors of Compiled Genealogies* (Boston: Newbury Street Press, 1998).

Krug, Steve. *Don't Make Me Think: A Common Sense Approach to Web Usability, Second Edition* (Indianapolis, Ind.: New Riders, 2006).

Mills, Elizabeth Shown. *Evidence! Citation & Analysis for the Family Historian* (Baltimore: Genealogical Publishing Co., 1997).

Mills, Elizabeth Shown, ed. *Professional Genealogy: A Manual for Researchers, Writers, Editors, Lecturers, and Librarians* (Baltimore: Genealogical Publishing Co., 2001).

Mulvaney, Nancy C. *Indexing Books*, 2nd ed. (Chicago: University of Chicago Press, 2005).

O'Conner, Patricia T. *Woe Is I: The Grammarphobe's Guide to Better English in Plain English*, 2nd ed. (New York: Riverhead Books, 2004).

Strunk, William, Jr., and E. B. White. *The Elements of Style*, 4th ed. (Boston: Allyn & Bacon, 1999).

Truss, Lynne. *Eats, Shoots & Leaves: The Zero Tolerance Approach to Punctuation!* (New York: Gotham Books, 2003).

Walsh, Bill. *Lapsing into a Comma: A Curmudgeon's Guide to the Many Things That Can Go Wrong in Print — and How to Avoid Them* (Lincolnwood [Chicago], Ill.: Contemporary Books, 2000).

Williams, Robin, and John Tollett. *The Non-Designer's Web Book*, 3rd ed. (Berkeley, Cal.: Peachpit Press, 2006).

INDEX